Heroes in Death

Heroes in Death
The von Blücher Brothers in the Fallschirmjäger
Crete, May 1941

Adrian Nisbett

SCHIFFER MILITARY HISTORY
Atglen, PA

Dedication

For the late Gertrud Freifrau von Ketelhodt (born Gräfin von Blücher), January 10, 1921 - December 18, 2013, whose great pride in her brothers never waned during her long life, and for my late parents, who instilled in me a lifelong love of books

Copyright © 2014 by Adrian Nisbett

Library of Congress Control Number: 2014932123

All rights reserved. No part of this work may be reproduced or used in any form or by any means—graphic, electronic, or mechanical, including photocopying or information storage and retrieval systems—without written permission from the publisher.

The scanning, uploading, and distribution of this book or any part thereof via the Internet or via any other means without the permission of the publisher is illegal and punishable by law. Please purchase only authorized editions and do not participate in or encourage the electronic piracy of copyrighted materials.
"Schiffer," "Schiffer Publishing, Ltd. & Design," and the "Design of pen and inkwell" are registered trademarks of Schiffer Publishing, Ltd.

Designed by Molly Shields
Type set in ITC Garamond Std/Adobe Garamond
ISBN: 978-0-7643-4631-6
Printed in China

Published by Schiffer Publishing, Ltd.
4880 Lower Valley Road
Atglen, PA 19310
Phone: (610) 593-1777; Fax: (610) 593-2002
E-mail: Info@schifferbooks.com

For our complete selection of fine books on this and related subjects, please visit our website at www.schifferbooks.com. You may also write for a free catalog.

This book may be purchased from the publisher. Please try your bookstore first.

We are always looking for people to write books on new and related subjects. If you have an idea for a book, please contact us at proposals@schifferbooks.com.

Schiffer Publishing's titles are available at special discounts for bulk purchases for sales promotions or premiums. Special editions, including personalized covers, corporate imprints, and excerpts can be created in large quantities for special needs. For more information, contact the publisher.

Contents

Prologue 6

Part One
Life Before War 16

Part Two
The Making of the Fallschirmjäger 40

Part Three
The Knight's Cross 61

Part Four
Crete 74

Part Five
Aftermath 124

Acknowledgements 171

Bibliography 175

Rank Equivalents 176

Prologue

Finally. The waiting had been a long test of mind and body, sitting in sticky 40°C heat beside a noisy runway, every few minutes encased in clouds of fine, powdery dust, strapped up with equipment, then unbuckling the gear and assisting *Luftwaffe* (Air Force) ground personnel to prepare the aircraft; and always the waiting. It was the lot of soldiers everywhere, for as long as there had been armies: the shouted orders to hurry up; the tense excitement of preparing for the operation; the endless questions in their minds – "Am I ready? Will I be able to jump? Will I do my job?" – and then the delays. Today, the 20th of May 1941, was the day the *Fallschirmjäger* (paratroopers) of the 1st Regiment would prove their worth and justify the swagger they adopted when on leave and wearing their much prized badges and boots. This was the day that they would show the world that the paratroopers could live up to the propaganda.

All the same, it cannot have been an encouraging sign to the less experienced and the superstitious among them to notice a large flock of vultures lining one side of the runway, in the land which made portent – reading by oracles into a lucrative if not always reliable profession.

So far, all that nervous tension had been drained by the relentless heat and the

Waiting to take off on the flight to Crete, paratroopers and aircrew seek shelter from the Greek sun under the Ju 52's broad wing. Courtesy of Paul Bernhard.

boredom, punctuated only by the refueling task, so that no matter what lay in store, it had to be better than Topolia airfield, a temporary airport north of Athens. For now, the men were reduced to watching the returning aircraft land, some of them damaged by anti-aircraft fire and others, too many, suffering mechanical problems.

At last the order came and they joined the lines of their comrades slowly boarding their "Auntie Ju." They walked awkwardly, restrained by numerous belts and straps securing the parachute and equipment, but unlike their Allied counterparts, they were not weighed down by an overload of gear. The parachute was a necessary burden, but

Work on the aircraft continued despite the heat. Note the covered cockpit and engines to provide protection from heat and dust. Courtesy Moog Collection.

otherwise the men carried only a holstered pistol on their waist belts, grenades, perhaps a sub-machine gun, a water-bottle and whatever personal items (many carried cameras) and emergency rations that could be crammed into the ample pockets of their jump smocks and uniforms.

The sixteen men on board could reflect not only on the day's delays and discomforts, but also on the long journey that had brought them to Greece. It had seemed an endless train trip through Eastern European countries, but the prospect of action had kept them keen and boisterous. Now, as the aircraft lifted hesitantly at first, then sturdily from the ground and the air began to cool, the men could turn their heads and look back on the makeshift airfield that had been their home for the past several weeks. The dramatic difference between where they had come from and where they had ended up could not have been more marked. From Stendal, the home of the German paratrooper, and from other bases and homes throughout Germany the men had been recalled hastily for the big operation. There had been great secrecy surrounding the mission and as they assembled at Stendal, near Berlin, they were ordered to remove any identifying insignia or pieces of uniform which would immediately set them apart as *Fallschirmjäger*. For men proud to belong to such an elite unit, this went against the grain. They were to remove the prized *Fallschirmspringerabzeichen* or qualification badge from their breasts and exchange the distinctive jump boots for standard *Luftwaffe* marching boots. All of their special pieces of equipment and

Crete bound Ju 52 at low level over the Sea of Crete.
Courtesy Moog Collection.

uniform were stowed in knapsacks and bags so that when they travelled they looked like any other *Luftwaffe* ground personnel.

Despite all the subterfuge and secrecy, the details of the operation, code-named *"Merkur"* (Mercury, after the Roman god, also known as Hermes, the winged messenger in Greek legend), would become known to the commanders of the Allied forces awaiting them, almost as soon as the plans reached their own leaders.

The journey had begun with a long train ride to Germany's frontier, then 1,000 kilometers or more in the back of teeth-rattling trucks or crowded trains travelling over roads many of which were little more than rutted wagon trails. It was a tiring and confusing trip, some 3,000 kilometers through recently conquered lands and friendly countries, like Hungary.

As they travelled, the veterans of Norway and Holland could reflect on memories of past jumps, some aspects of which would have been firmly pushed into the deeper parts of their minds, while their younger comrades looked toward the mission with a mixture of excitement, anticipation and fear. Despite these mixed feelings the men were full of confidence. They had prevailed in all their actions to date, despite some heavy losses. Now they were to take part in the big one, the first great airborne invasion in history.

Once the men had arrived at their staging areas – mostly dirt airstrips north of Athens – and disembarked they could become paratroopers once again. The physical training resumed, weapons were tested and cleaned, and tactics were reviewed. Shortly after they arrived in

Greece came the news they had waited for. They learned their target would be the island of Crete. German intelligence predicted that the island was guarded by fewer than 5,000 Allied troops and that the shock of a large-scale airborne assault, supported by mountain troops arrivving by air and by reinforcements arriving from the sea, would overwhelm an already defeated Allied force. This force, a mixture of British, Australian, New Zealand and Greek infantry supported by assorted service units and some artillery batteries and tank squadrons had recently been ignominiously thrown out of Greece. Intelligence was certain that this was nothing more than a demoralized and poorly led opposition. Furthermore, the paratroop commanders were assured that the people of Crete resented having Allied troops on their island and would greet the paratroopers as liberators. No doubt some of the veterans thought it all sounded too easy, but their leaders were radiating confidence and doubts were not welcomed among the tough men of the 7th *Flieger* Division of XI *FliegerKorps*.

For the men of the 1st *Fallschirmjäger* Regiment the mission was at once challenging and straightforward. The 1st Battalion would drop on the eastern side of Heraklion airport and take the Gournes radio station while the 2nd Battalion would drop on the western side and storm the airport. The 1st Battalion would then push forward to the airport and link up with the 2nd Battalion with the combined force providing support for the 3rd Battalion, tasked with taking the adjoining town and port of Heraklion. The secured airfield would allow the Ju 52s to carry in heavy weapons and more strongly armed ground troops, who would then fan out and begin to take control of the surrounding country. Capturing the town of Heraklion would present the Germans with the best port on Crete. This was the straightforward mission of the Eastern group; the Western and Centre groups were similarly tasked with taking airfields and ports along the northern coast of Crete, at Maleme, Chania (now Canea) and Rethymnon.

In the days, weeks and years following the operation, those men from the 1st and 2nd battalions who survived the next twenty-four hours would no doubt have discussed and reflected upon the hell they had been dropped into. So many of their comrades were to die in the first day that the two battalions were almost spent as fighting forces. That they eventually prevailed says more about the quality of the individual *Fallschirmjäger* than it does about the intelligence and staff work which failed so conspicuously. In retrospect, there were many warning signs that this would be far from an easy operation. The usually meticulous German planning and staff work had fallen down in several vital areas. As a result the men, who had prepared themselves to be transported into battle in the early afternoon were still sitting in the hot sun as the day was ending. Every aircraft which took off from the makeshift airfields churned up great clouds of dust. Apart from slowing the progress of the airlift, the dust clouded into the eyes, noses, ears and weapons of the already sweating paratroopers. The heat and the dust added extreme discomfort to an already miserable wait for them, made worse by the unsettling and demeaning order to discard all of their equipment and assist in the refueling of aircraft as they returned from their early runs to Crete. As the day progressed the problems multiplied and departure times were pushed back hour-by-hour. Some returning aircraft were damaged and crash-landed. They had to be moved from the airstrip before aircraft could take off or land. The dust clouds delayed flight after flight. In the end the regiment had to leave behind 600 men on that first day, simply because there were not enough transports left to get them there in daylight hours. The regimental commander, *Oberst* Bruno Bräuer, was as impatient as his men to get underway and his decision to leave those 600 men behind would be yet another piece of kindling for the fiery near-disaster which lay ahead.

By the time the first of the regiment's aircraft took off for the ninety minute flight the scheduled departure time of 13:00 hours had long since passed. It would be closer to 18:00 hours before the first men jumped and the planned mass drop would no longer be possible. The lack of aircraft meant that they would be dropped in much smaller groups than originally intended, making the trademark paratroop tactic of an overwhelming and swift assault on the enemy almost impossible to achieve. Still, they were *Fallschirmjäger* and the impossible was just a challenge. Most of the men sat on the bench seats along the fuselage of the aircraft in silence. There was some half-hearted singing of "*Rot scheint die Sonne*" (Red shines the Sun), the *Fallschirmjäger* marching song, but for the most part the exhausted and apprehensive men were content to sit in their own worlds and simply appreciate the opportunity to be away from dust and in a slightly cooler atmosphere. Some of them no doubt looked out the windows and as the aircraft cruised at not much more than 200 kilometers per hour (130 mph) they were treated to very low level views of the blue-black Sea of Crete and its islands which emerged so dramatically from the waters and were so steeped in mystery and myth: Milos, Mykonos, Santorini. The veterans may have wondered about the terrain of Crete after seeing these islands: rocky, steep and forbidding.

Among the men of the 1st Battalion were two brothers. *Oberleutnant* Wolfgang von Blücher was twenty-four years old and already a hero of the regiment. He had jumped into Norway in April 1940, where he had earned the Iron Cross First and Second Class. Then he took part in the assault on the Dordrecht bridges in Holland, where his daring and bravery in leading a night assault earned him the Knight's Cross. Following that operation he returned to Norway in June to fight at Narvik. Serving with the brother he idolized was seventeen year-old Hans Joachim. He had pleaded with his mother at every opportunity to allow him be with his two older brothers and to join the *Fallschirmjäger*. At last she had given way and Hans Joachim (known as Jochen to family and friends) had been given special accelerated training to allow him to join his brothers. A third brother, nineteen year-old Lebrecht was serving in the 2nd Battalion as a *Gefreiter* (lance-corporal – see equivalent American/British ranks at the end of the book). For Lebrecht and Jochen this was their first combat jump. While there must have been some

A studio portrait of Wolfgang, taken after the award of his Knight's Cross in 1940. Courtesy Gertrud v. Ketelhodt.

comfort in the knowledge that they were going into action with their heroic brother, behind the brave faces and ready smiles there was no doubt much apprehension and uncertainty. They were members of one of Germany's most illustrious military families and each carried the title *Graf* (Count), but in the *Fallschirmjäger* there were no quick promotions to officer status for such men: they had to earn every rank, just like everyone else in the regiment.

The men of the *Fallschirmjäger* battalions were the cream of the German Armed Forces. They were all volunteers who had met a stringent set of entry requirements, were physically and mentally tough and were trained to a very high level in the style of warfare for which paratroopers were best suited: quick decisive assaults carried out with unhesitating aggression and unflagging élan. They were confident and they had every reason to be so. Just as the briefings had emphasized the weakness of the Allied forces waiting for them the men had total confidence in both their own ability and in that of the officers leading them. The regiment was full of veterans of previous campaigns and with that very firm backbone there would have been little reason for any of the men to have felt any qualms about this mission. In fact, there was only one man who expressed doubt about the operation but was persuaded by one of his favorite generals to allow it to go ahead: Adolf Hitler. He believed that the paratroopers would meet with very heavy casualties and that victory was by no means guaranteed. Hitler was convinced to approve the operation by *General der Flieger* Kurt Student, the man who had built up the *7th Flieger Division* from scratch. He had almost single-handedly developed the culture and doctrine of the *Fallschirmjäger* and had led the division in its early actions (and was severely wounded during the invasion of the Netherlands); he was determined that this assault would prove once and for all the value of his airborne troops. But for now, the planning over, all he could do was sit in his headquarters (recently vacated by the British Army commanders) in the Hotel Grand Bretagne on Syntagma Square in Athens and await news of victory.

As the aircraft carrying the 1st and 2nd Battalions approached the island of Crete they climbed to their required height of 200 meters to clear high terrain surrounding the jump zones (much higher than the usual jump height of 120 meters, which was designed to get the men on the ground as quickly as possible) and as the Junkers banked hard to the right for the run into Heraklion airport the men on board stood and prepared themselves to leap from the aircraft. The tri-motored Ju 52s slowed from an already lumbering 200 kilometers per hour to allow the men to jump safely, the men made a final check of their harnesses and static lines, began shuffling to the door and prepared to jump headfirst into action. They would have been all too conscious of a maelstrom of fire coming towards them: exploding anti-aircraft shells sending jagged shards of metal through the thin aluminum fuselages; partial views of aircraft trailing fire and smoke; rounds from smaller caliber rifles and machine-guns zipping through the cabin, occasionally finding human flesh with a solid "thump"; the aircraft bouncing and rolling despite the pilots' efforts to stay straight and level for the jump. But they were Fallschirmjäger: they would jump.

Junkers Ju 52s on the way to Crete. Courtesy Moog Collection.

On the ground, other men waited, many thousands more in total than German intelligence had predicted. They knew exactly what was coming. They had had plenty of time to prepare their positions, and now as the bombing raids ended and the transports approached them, they felt confident that they could beat off the German assault. As German intelligence had reported, this was a defeated force. But its morale had been strengthened and numbers increased during its time on Crete and with sufficient time to build strong defensive positions the combined Allied force prepared to shoot the low-flying aircraft and their human cargo out of the sky. As the first aircraft passed over the airport in parallel with Australian troops manning defensive positions on the cone-shaped hills near the airport known as the Two Charlies, the Australians were astonished to see that the aircraft were flying almost level with their eyes. Their astonishment turned to awe as the black figures jumping from the aircraft suddenly blossomed into hundreds of white parachutes. Then the Australians started shooting with everything they had.

There was no going back. The greatest airborne assault in history was underway. The von Blücher brothers were about to descend into a fight so grim, bloody and unforgiving that the very existence of the *Fallschirmjäger* regiments would soon be called into question.

"*Glück Ab!*" The men called the paratroopers' greeting to each other. "Have a good jump!"

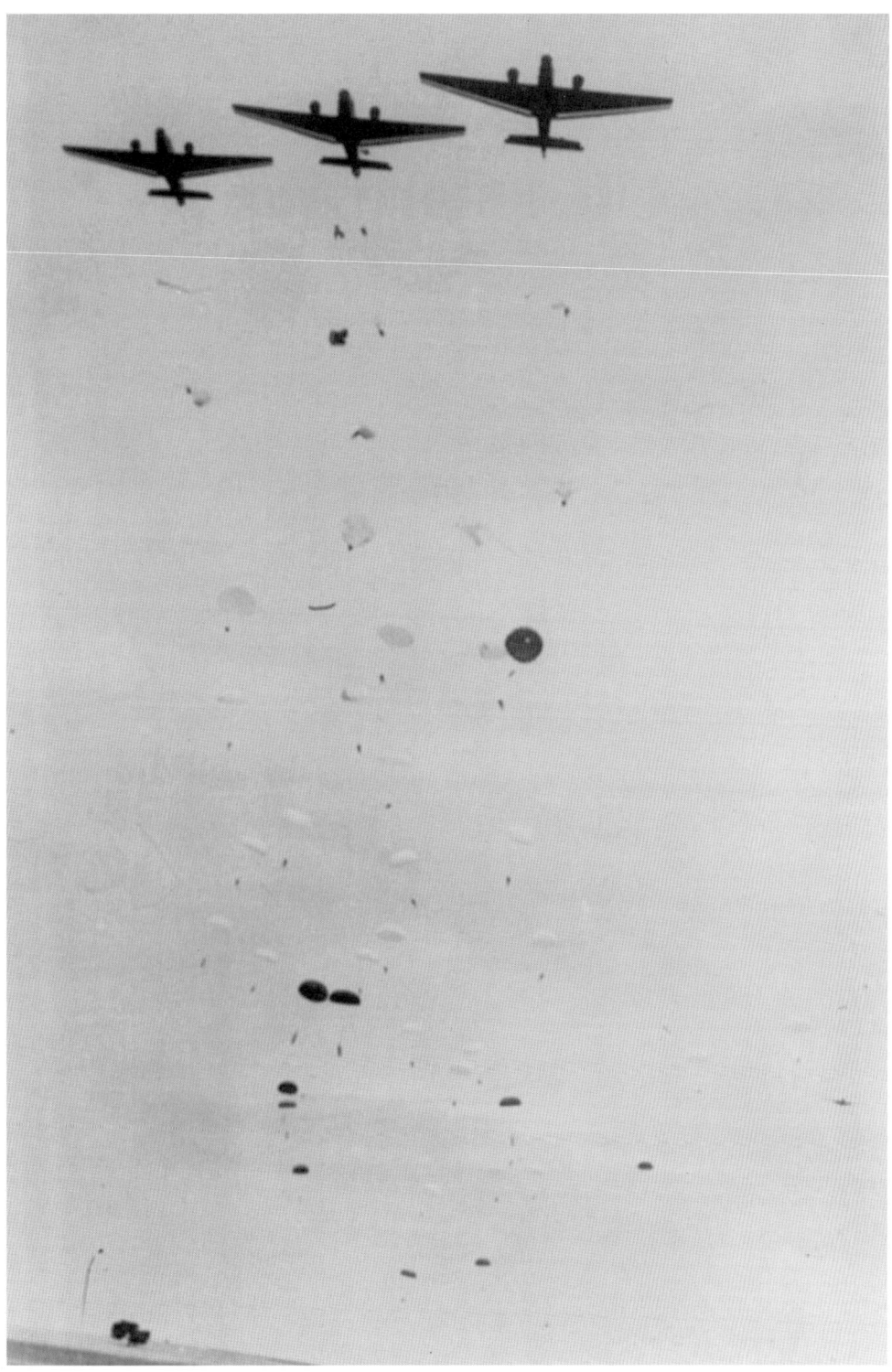

Operation Merkur begins as the first units jump over the Heraklion area. Courtesy Moog Collection.

Part One
Life Before War

The small village of Fincken, population about 200, is situated midway between Berlin (150 kilometers to the south) and Rostock (100 kilometers to the north) in the Mecklenburg lakes district; it has existed as a named village for over 700 years. The village is surrounded by rich farmland and forests and is well off the main roads which link the larger towns and cities. However, only the very impressive round barn (built as a horse stable), a large and solid circular building now serving as a cleverly designed multi-purpose community center, but retaining its mid-19th century outer wall, suggests that this village has existed for centuries. Along the main street the centuries-old links to the land are emphasized by the pastures which run right up to the back doors of some of the houses. There is a small *gasthof* amid the houses, but there are no permanent shops, only a travelling caravan which appears once a week and sells a small selection of groceries and drinks. On the other side of the street and extending for several hundred meters runs an old stone wall which once protected the extensive groves of trees, meadows and gardens belonging to the *schloss* (castle or

The main house and early home of the von Blücher family at Fincken, c.1914. Courtesy Gertrud v. Ketelhodt.

country manor), once the home of the von Blücher family and which still stands near the head of the road which brings visitors into Fincken. Still much as it was a century ago, the several hectares of land provide a delightful short walk between the manor house and the family chapel with its adjoining graveyard. On this extensive stretch of grass, shrubs and trees between the road and the lake it is not difficult to get a feel for the comfortable and beautiful surroundings that the von Blüchers enjoyed. Beyond the land immediately adjoining the *schloss*, most of the old houses have been extensively renovated and much newer cottages have been built near the lake. In direct line of sight from the front of the *schloss* is a block of flats built during the Communist era (Fincken was part of the former East Germany). This extremely ugly building is unfortunately very close to the round barn and to the *schloss* and its associated buildings.

Despite neglect in recent years and the erection nearby of less grand buildings, the *schloss* still retains its dominant position at the entrance to the village. The house, for 120 years home to the von Blücher family, was built in 1801 and enlarged in 1850. In contrast to the situation in other German states, estate owners in Mecklenburg retained considerable powers over the local population until the early 19th century. Serfdom was abolished only in 1820 and even in the first decade of the 20th century the Count exerted strong influence over the affairs of Fincken and the nearby villages of Darze and Käselin, where there were other von Blücher estates.

Though stripped of most of its former grandeur, the house was still in good order in 1990. Courtesy Lebrecht v. Blücher.

The house in 2012, derelict and waiting for a new lease of life. The building is in need of serious renovation and repair. Author photo.

By the early 20th century, however, the von Blücher family was not cash rich. *Graf* (Count) Adolf von Blücher had little real experience in farming and relied heavily on his excellent estate manager to keep the land productive and profitable. Despite the estate manager's expertise, the early death of *Graf* Adolf in 1924 and Germany's economic woes in the 1920s and early-1930s changed the family's standing in Fincken irrevocably. In 1932 the *schloss* was transformed into a residence for retirees. Since 1945, when the family was forced to flee ahead of the advancing Russian army, the large country house has been a refugee center, a youth resort and a hotel. In its various guises it has undergone many changes and today the interior is drably dressed in 1960s blond wood and the starkly designed fittings of a Soviet-era hotel. Only in the vast cellars which fill the entire area under the house are there reminders of the past. The servant rooms, doorless cells really, are still there, as are the food and wine storage rooms, an old bowling alley and some rusted metal pulleys whose purpose is not clear. Above ground, there is little to suggest that once this was the center of life in the village, from where the *Graf* would keep watch on the farmhands working the surrounding land, and where disputes would be settled and problems resolved. The outbuildings, stables, storerooms and workers' quarters still stand, but the gardens have been allowed to run wild and the outer walls of the *schloss* are beginning to crumble. There are no polished wooden window frames or finely carved doors now, just long wearing aluminum frames; even worse is the fire resistant eyesore which replaced the original and reportedly quite magnificent staircase and entrance hall. At least the views from the windows give some idea of what it must have been like to live there in the *schloss*'s heyday,

The old von Blücher family chapel, located a hundred meters from the house. The chapel was recently restored and is in excellent condition. Author photo.

as they reach across to the lake at the bottom of the gardens and over what were once extensive groves and terraces. Of the family which once lived there, nothing tangible remains. The finely proportioned rooms, with wood paneling and decorative ceilings are no more. Most of the upstairs rooms have been partitioned into small bedrooms, while downstairs the reception and lounge rooms and other living areas have been reshaped to meet the requirements of a country hotel.

For reminders of the von Blücher family's presence you have to leave the house and walk the hundred meters or so through long grass and overgrown gardens to the small church (built in 1748) and its quiet and beautifully maintained yard. Inside the restored chapel the coat of arms of the von Blücher family still has pride of place in front of the pulpit and above the front door. In the churchyard, slightly apart from the graves of other village residents, lie two members of the family, *Graf* Adolf, who died in 1924 and his son, also *Graf* Adolf, whose death in 1944 brought to an end the male line of this branch of the

The elaborately decorated pulpit inside the chapel, displaying the von Blücher coat of arms. Author photo.

family. There is also a marble plaque which reminds visitors of a family tragedy in a faraway place, earlier in the war years.

Once the most important family in the district, nowadays the von Blüchers are mostly forgotten in the village. There are some older residents who remember the family before and during the war, but for most villagers the family's history and even their name are of no consequence to their lives in the 21st century. As with many parts of the former East Germany, Fincken has not found an economic miracle and it exists today largely as it has for centuries, through its farms. Young people have drifted to the larger towns and cities for work and the visitor senses that for all its pride in its long existence, Fincken is still searching for a way to the future. Situated as it is among lakes and forests, the future may lie in tourism more than farming and it is just possible that the *schloss* will one day come back to life and perhaps even take on some of the grandeur and style of its early 20th century life.

It was at Fincken, in the Mecklenburg district, that *Graf* Adolf Theodor Wolfgang Constantin Lebrecht von Blücher was born on 17 September 1883. The Fincken branch of the von Blücher family, descended from *Graf* Adolf (1821-1875) is several branches removed from the Marshal von Blücher of Waterloo fame, but military service was to be a popular family occupation through the following generations. During the First World War, five family members fell and in the Second World War sixteen were to die.

Graf Adolf attended a *gymnasium* in Doberan, then studied law in Lausanne and Berlin. In 1905 he became a cadet officer in the Hussar Regiment von Ziethen and was promoted to lieutenant in 1906 and captain in 1913. In that year he was granted a leave of absence and began farming on the family estate. At the outbreak of war in August 1914 he was appointed adjutant of the regiment, then based in Kurland. For a time he led a squadron of Dragoons in Poland, then commanded an infantry unit on the Western Front. He was awarded the Iron Cross, First and Second class.

In August 1914, Adolf, then a *Rittmeister* (cavalry captain) of his regiment, married *Freiin* (Baroness) Gertrud Marschall von Altengottern. Their marriage produced six children, beginning with *Gräfin* (Countess) Elisabeth (who died in April 2012) in 1915. The first son, *Graf* Wolfgang, was born in 1917, followed by *Graf* Adolf (1918), *Gräfin* Gertrud (1921), *Graf* Lebrecht (1922) and *Graf* Hans Joachim (1923). His ever-increasing family must have placed considerable pressure on Adolf as he struggled to make his estate profitable, amid Germany's post-First World War economic upheavals. Despite the presence of his very competent farm manager, he met with limited success and in April 1924, Adolf contracted influenza and died suddenly from the infection and heart disease. His sudden death left a large and very young family fatherless and in a very difficult financial situation. Their material fortune was very much tied to the farmlands and forests around the family home and the lack of readily available cash caused considerable hardship. Difficult times followed, despite *Freiin* Gertrud's marriage in 1928 to the estate manager, Ludwig von Nordheim. By December 1931 the estates at Fincken and Knüppeldamm had been lost and in the midst of world economic turmoil the family moved to the recently purchased estate of Neetze, near Lüneburg. The remaining family estates at Käselin and Darze (both near Fincken and legally owned by the *Graf*'s male heirs, his sons) were being managed by the von Blücher boys' legal guardian (appointed by the state) and a local inspector of agriculture. As the world depression deepened and hit an already economically weakened Germany, more hardship struck the family in 1933, when the Neetze estate was also lost. The family then moved in with *Freiin* Gertrud's parents in Altengottern and Ludwig von Nordheim was employed by the *Luftwaffe* as a farmer. Thereafter, until towards the end of the war the family

Adolf Graf von Blücher with Wolfgang (L) and Elisabeth in 1918.
Courtesy Gertrud v. Ketelhodt.

lived in a succession of homes in Munich, Braunschweig, Münster and Posen. Before and during the war, Wolfgang and later Adolf managed their inherited farms near Fincken, thus maintaining the family's link to its traditional land.

As the war turned against Germany and the Russians advanced, *Freiin* Gertrud von Nordheim was forced to move several more times. In January 1945 she left Posen and found shelter with her sister Charlotte in the village of Mecklenburg. In April they were on the move again, this time to Schleswig-Holstein, in Celle. By September she was living with her second daughter, Gertrud, and had received news that her husband, Ludwig, was being held as a prisoner-of-war by the Russians. Worse news soon followed:

Freifrau Gertrud von Ketelhodt (née von Blücher) in 2012. Author photo.

she learned in 1951 that he had been sentenced to twenty-five years of forced labor, a punishment which was commuted in 1953 only after the intervention of German Chancellor Konrad Adenauer.

The six von Blücher children were forced to live a rather nomadic existence, therefore, for most of their young years. Despite this, all were well educated and somehow the money was found to send both boys and girls to boarding schools. In addition, holidays were spent at in the country at Fincken or Altengottern (their maternal grandparents' estate) and the children relished the freedom to roam and explore, enjoying activities largely unknown to those who lived in towns and cities.

In adulthood, Elisabeth trained as a

Gertrud's first husband, Colonel Georg Michael. Courtesy Lebrecht v. Blücher.

child-care supervisor and married Hubert von Puttkamer in 1967. During the war she had worked as a secretary in the manor houses at Darze and Käselin and in April 1945 fled Käselin with her sister-in-law *Gräfin* Gisela (widow of *Graf* Adolf, who had died in 1944) in a horse-drawn carriage. Younger sister Gertrud studied photography in Berlin and in 1941 married Colonel Georg Michael, a holder of the Knight's Cross (awarded in January 1941) with Oak Leaves (awarded in January 1943, for extreme bravery and leadership in action). He was a Panzer Grenadier officer who, in addition to his Knight's Cross had been awarded both levels of the

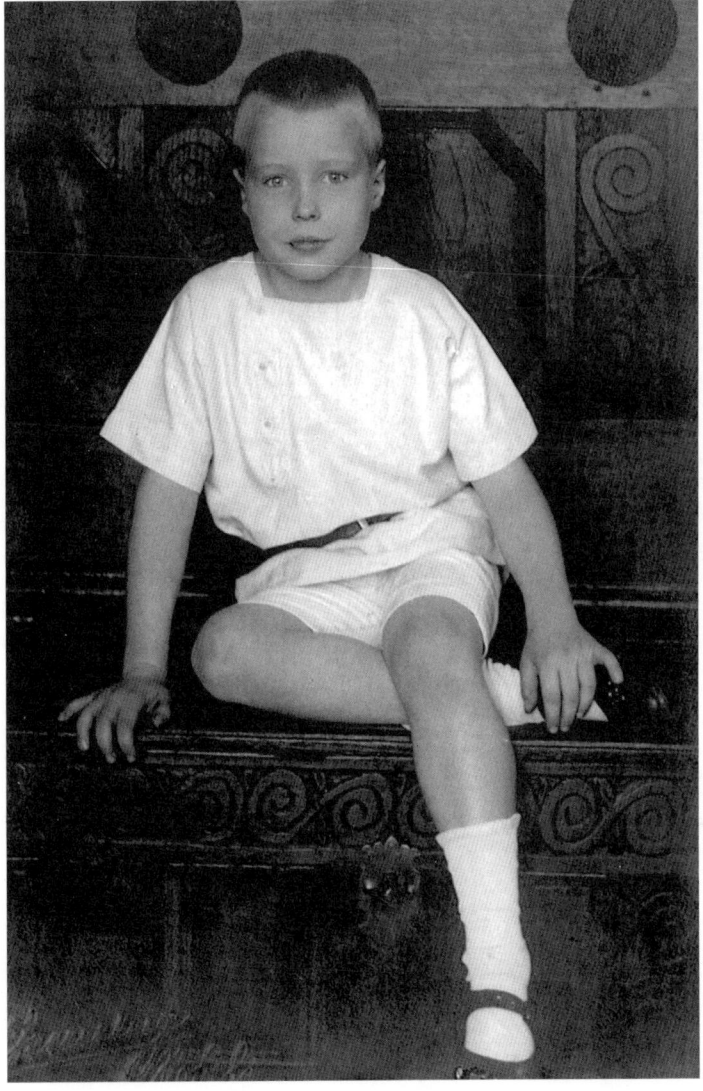

Wolfgang in 1924, aged seven. Courtesy Gertrud v. Ketelhodt.

Iron Cross, two Tank Destruction badges in Silver and a gold Wound Badge. He served in Poland, France and Russia, where he died of wounds received in action while commanding the 2nd Battalion of the 26th Panzer Grenadier Regiment at Dujoprovka, Nikolpol in January 1944. He was twenty-six years old when he died. Like her sister Elisabeth, Gertrud was forced to flee as the Russian army advanced and with her two young daughters reached Lage where she stayed with her father-in-law.

The eldest son, Wolfgang, attended the local primary school in Fincken, then received lessons at home from a private teacher. He and his brothers and sisters

The lake behind the house at Fincken in 2012, as idyllic a spot today as it was when the von Blücher children played there in the 1920s and 1930s. Author photo.

must have enjoyed a wonderful few years living in the extensive grounds at Fincken. The gardens provided ample areas for play, but the lake at the back door would have been the real attraction, as it provided opportunities for a variety of adventures, as well as swimming, sailing and fishing. Despite this idyllic world for children, Gertrud remembers that when the family was still at Fincken they actually lived in a smaller house nearby, as they could not afford the upkeep of the big house. The children all learned to swim at young ages and they spent many hours in the outdoors. Their mother insisted that each day they were to take a walk for at least one hour, regardless of the weather. The children grew up close to nature and early on learned skills like boating and horse riding. According to Gertrud, growing up in a rural environment meant a rather less regimented atmosphere than that experienced by children from towns and cities and this tended to compensate for the harsh disciplinary regime of the boarding schools which all the children attended.

After the local school at Fincken, Wolfgang then attended the Baltic School, at Misdroy (now Miedzyzdroje in Poland) as a boarder from 1929 to 1931. He completed his schooling at the Hermann-Billung School in Celle. After school and feeling great responsibility as the oldest male in the family, Wolfgang studied farming and forestry with the aim of creating a stable home at Darze for his mother and brothers and sisters. He took his position as breadwinner and surrogate father very seriously, so much so that at sixteen he announced to the family that he was going to leave school and get a job so that he could support the family. One of Gertrud's strongest memories of Wolfgang is his determination to take responsibility and his mental and physical toughness, traits that obviously helped make him a fine young officer.

In 1935 Wolfgang followed his father's example and joined a reserve cavalry regiment in Rathenow. At the same time he became an agricultural officer in Mecklenburg and worked for a further two years in an agricultural trust office in Rostock. Thereafter he worked on estates in Hinrichshagen and Mustin with the aim of becoming a forester. In 1938 he was promoted to the rank of *Leutnant* in the army reserve. In early 1939 he requested transfer to the *Luftwaffe* to be trained as a fighter pilot. Unfortunately, due to an illness at the time he was found at the aeronautical medical examination in March to be "temporarily unfit." However, his transfer had been approved and it was felt by his superiors that in a matter of several months he would be fit to begin flying training.

At some point in those months, Wolfgang decided to join the *Fallschirmjäger* Regiment. According to Gertrud, he wanted to see action, to travel and to learn new skills. Interestingly, his first application was rejected, but "in view of the changed circumstances" (no doubt the outbreak of war in September), Wolfgang's application was re-submitted and in January 1940 he joined the First Parachute Regiment, based at Stendal. By April 1940 he was in action in Norway, for which he was awarded the Iron Cross First and Second Class. On 10 May 1940 he and his platoon jumped near Dordrecht in Holland. His exploits here, for which he received the Knight's Cross, are described in more detail in Part Three. In June he was back in Norway, taking part in the fighting at Narvik and Oslo. Having seen a lot of action in a short time, Wolfgang took an extended leave in the autumn of 1940 and returned to manage the forests at Darze and Käselin. While at home he spoke of his love for the paratroop regiment, with its strong comradeship and dramatic missions. The other children and their mother were, of course, extremely proud of Wolfgang and his awards; Gertrud recalled how honored they felt to receive phone calls from officials in Berlin, congratulating the family on having such a fine son. Younger brothers Lebrecht and Hans Joachim were entranced by the stories of Wolfgang's experiences and it would be only a matter of time before they too followed him into the paratroops.

The second oldest brother, Adolf, like Wolfgang, spent his first three school years at the local primary school in Fincken. After some home schooling, he went to the *gymnasium* at Plau/Mecklenburg, then from 1931 attended the Hermann-Billung School in Celle, where he completed his *Abitur* (matriculation) in 1937. After six months of compulsory service for the *Reichsarbeitdienst* (the national labor office, which administered a form of national service, often in agriculture, for young

(L-R) Adolf, an unidentified cousin, Wolfgang, Richenza von Nordheim (stepsister), at Fincken in 1930, when Wolfgang was thirteen. Courtesy Gertrud v. Ketelhodt.

Germans) he joined the *Kriegsmarine* (Navy) as an officer cadet in the autumn of 1937. During his training he made overseas cruises aboard the sailing ship (training) "*Horst Wessel*" and the liner "*Schlesien*." He was promoted to *Leutnant zur See* (lieutenant) and began training as a naval aviator at Parow (Pomerania). Adolf served with a coastal patrol squadron in northern France, during which time he was awarded the Iron Cross First and Second Class. He was promoted to First Lieutenant in 1941.

Lebrecht (often called Lebs in the family), the third son, was born in Fincken in 1922. In 1928 he began his education as his brothers had, at the local primary school. He then moved to the Johanneum in Lüneburg and from 1933 he attended the Hermann-Billung School in Celle, like his older brothers. He completed his *Abitur* in 1940, having been a very strong student in science and languages with a definite bent towards engineering as a career. He also loved German literature, listening to music and playing musical instruments. Like his brothers he was a very keen water sportsman and a good athlete. After he completed school he tried to join the *Kriegsmarine*, but was rejected due to an eye weakness. Lebrecht then completed his compulsory *Arbeitsdienst* service and afterwards joined the army as an officer cadet senior grade (*Fahnenjunker*) with the 94th Infantry Regiment at Köslin.

Adolf in his naval officer's uniform in 1939. Courtesy Lebrecht v. Blücher.

Lebrecht in 1924, aged two. Courtesy Gertrud v. Ketelhodt.

(L-R) Hubertus von Marschall (cousin), Lebrecht and Hans Joachim at Altengottern (their maternal grandparents' estate), c.1931. Courtesy Gertrud v. Ketelhodt.

He was not long there, however, before his brother Wolfgang suggested he join the paratroopers. He was immediately accepted and began training, joining the Second Battalion of the First Parachute Regiment (7th company) at Tangermünde on 21 April 1941. He was promoted to *Gefreiter* in May 1941, just before the Crete operation.

Adolf and Gertrud's youngest child was Hans Joachim (known as Jochen to family and friends), who was born on 23 October 1923, in Fincken. Like his brothers he was blond, well-built and of average height, with a natural inclination towards sports and outdoor activities. His sister Gertrud

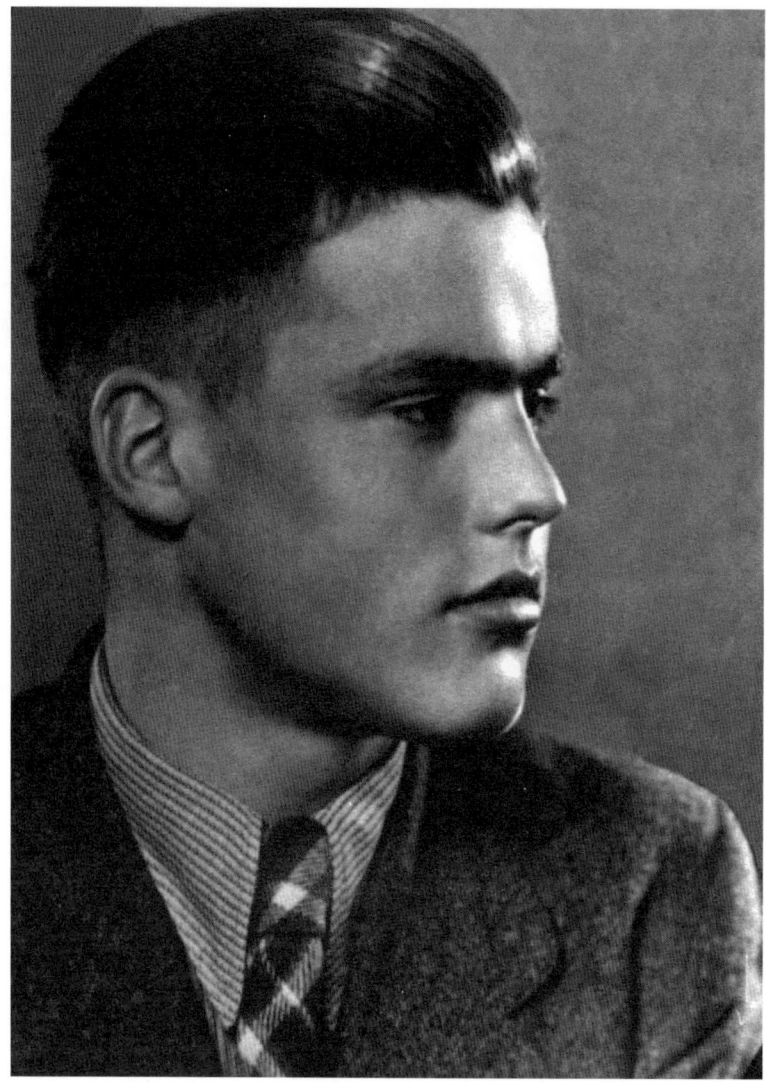

A studio portrait of Lebrecht, taken in Celle in 1939, when he was seventeen. Courtesy of Gertrud v. Ketelhodt.

described him as a "born athlete" who always cared more about others than himself. He attended primary schools in Fincken, Neetze and Altengottern, then high school at *gymnasiums* in Hannover and Münster as the family moved homes, before going to the Baltic School in Misdroy as a boarder. Here he was a strong student and very highly regarded; he was renowned for his physical and mental strength and for his natural athletic talent. He was proud of these qualities, but he was also very supportive of family and friends and he stood up for anyone he felt was being unfairly treated. This trait, together with his courage to the point of

Hans Joachim (Jochen) in 1924, aged one year. Courtesy Gertrud v. Ketelhodt.

Hans Joachim, aged eleven, wearing his Deutsche Jungvolk uniform, summer 1934. Courtesy Gertrud v. Ketelhodt.

fearlessness, was to cause him difficulties at the Baltic School, as his readiness to defend his schoolmates brought him into conflict with teachers. He was perhaps headstrong, but he was also capable of self-reflection, warmth and great loyalty, all qualities he showed at school and in his short military career. Certainly, his boarding housemaster thought most highly of him (see Aftermath) and by the time Hans Joachim left to join his brothers in the paratroops, they were warm friends.

Wolfgang had also attended the Baltic School, between 1929 and 1931. The school

Hans Joachim, aged twelve, riding his bike at Altengottern in 1935. Courtesy Gertrud v. Ketelhodt.

had been established in 1919 at the resort town of Misdroy, on the Baltic coast. It quickly attained a good reputation and became popular with families who lived east of the Elbe. The school had a strong athletic and sports emphasis, but also prided itself on producing "gentlemen." Though slated to be nationalized in 1944, more dramatic events overtook this decision and the school was closed as the approaching Russian armies neared the area. The school re-opened after the war as the Carl-Hunnius-Internat in Wyk but closed for good in 1959.

Whatever attractions the Baltic School held for Hans Joachim, all he really wanted to do was to serve alongside his brother Wolfgang, whom he idolized. Over many months he pleaded with his mother to allow him to join the *Fallschirmjäger* and despite her opposition

(L-R) Wolfgang, Elisabeth, Gertrud, Adolf, Hans Joachim, Richenza v. Nordheim, Lebrecht at Altengottern in 1934. Courtesy Gertrud v. Ketelhodt.

and strong misgivings, eventually she agreed. No doubt Wolfgang's standing in the regiment allowed him to pull strings with his superiors, because Hans Joachim was immediately accepted into the 1st Paratroop Regiment at only seventeen and without any prior military experience. He received accelerated training at Stendal during March 1941 and completed this in time to join his brothers for the invasion of Crete. He was posted to the 1st Battalion of the First Parachute Regiment, Wolfgang's unit, and joined the 1st company. Just as he had at school, Hans Joachim quickly established himself within the battalion. *Major* Erich Walther, his battalion commander, noted in his condolence letter to the family: "The youngster became in such a short time the favorite of us all; he longed ardently for battle and was blissfully

(L-R) Lebrecht, Adolf (in his naval cadet uniform), Elisabeth, Richenza v. Nordheim, Gertrud, Hans Joachim, Wolfgang in 1937. Courtesy Gertrud v. Ketelhodt.

happy when it finally began."

In reflecting on her brothers' short lives, Gertrud observed that in fact they never really had their own lives; Lebrecht and Hans Joachim were still just boys when they joined their older brother in the paratroops and from that point on they gave themselves to the service of their country. Were they Nazis or sympathetic to the Nazi cause? We will never know for sure, but according to Gertrud, they were not. She described Wolfgang as a farmer doing his duty. Of course, he became a soldier of some renown and distinction, but Gertrud maintains that he felt that he was simply serving his country, doing what was expected of one of his age, social class and family background. There is no doubt that he performed his duty as a paratrooper with dedication, commitment and considerable ability, but as a loyal German rather than a Nazi. The two younger boys were members of the *Deutsche Jungvolk* (the organization for children too young to join the Hitler Youth) and later the *Hitler Jugend* (Youth), but such membership certainly did not mean that the individual would eventually become a member of the Party or even sympathies with the Party. Gertrud says that the brothers showed no interest in politics at all, that they were all Christians who attended church regularly and that when they listened to the radio it was to music

Wolfgang in Luftwaffe uniform, with his horse on a family estate in February 1941. Courtesy Gertrud v. Ketelhodt.

rather than news that they were tuned. She recalls that their maternal grandmother, Baroness Wilhelmine Marschall von Altengottern (born *Gräfin* von Rittberg), exerted a considerable influence on her grandchildren. She instilled in them the importance of self-discipline and their obligation to accept responsibility. She had grown up in Germany's imperial age, when the aristocracy still had some standing in society and it would be natural for her to have instilled in her grandchildren the values and standards with which she had grown up. By the time of the Third Reich, although the aristocracy no longer had any influence on government, men of the von Blüchers' social standing remained very patriotic and still felt a responsibility to serve their country as their ancestors had. According to Gertrud, these qualities are crucial in understanding what motivated Wolfgang and his brothers: they understood their responsibility to family and Fatherland and exercised it without question. For Wolfgang, responsibility for his family had directed his life from the age of sixteen; Gertrud remembers that he accepted this responsibility not as a burden but with enthusiasm.

For a young sister who rarely saw her brothers, as they were frequently away from home at boarding school or in military service, the occasion of Hans Joachim's confirmation at Münster in 1939, when he was fifteen, shines in Gertrud's memory. It was to be the last time that the whole family would gather together.

At this distance in time and circumstance it is, of course, impossible to be certain about

(L-R) Richenza v. Nordheim, Hans Joachim, Lebrecht, Elisabeth, Gertrud, Wolfgang, Adolf, c.1931. Courtesy Gertrud v. Ketelhodt.

their political beliefs, if these existed at all. Lebrecht and Hans Joachim appear to have been motivated by their admiration for their older brother, rather than by any political factor. Like young men of any generation, they were heavily influenced, no doubt, by the distinction of being a paratrooper, by the adventuresome life that beckoned, by their sense of duty, by a youthful desire for action, but most of all by Wolfgang and his stories of his adventures in Norway and Holland. As brothers they were very close and without a father's guidance Lebrecht and Hans Joachim would have looked to Wolfgang as an example. Of course, at that early stage of the war, when a quick victory for Germany still seemed possible, all three (and their brother Adolf) would have seen military service as a temporary diversion in their paths to becoming farmers or engineers.

Part Two
The Making of the Fallschirmjäger

An information sheet for potential Fallschirmjäger, c.1939. Courtesy Fallschirmjäger archive, military archives, Freiburg. All photos and documents from this collection are in Files BW 57/484 and 57/485.

Information Sheet for voluntary entry into the *Fallschirm-Jäger-Rgt. 1 Stendal*

(1st Parachute Infantry Regiment in a Light Division, Stendal)

The recruitment of volunteers to the Fallschirm-Jäger-Rgt. 1 takes place on 1.10 each year.

1. The term of service is two years. In case of a corresponding eligibility for junior leadership, an additional duty of up to a total of 12 years is possible.

2. The uniform of the regiment is the same as that of the air force, with yellow color on the uniform and a bright green stripe bearing the inscription *"Fallschirm-Jäger-Rgt.-1."*

3. Volunteers between the ages of 17 and 22 are recruited. Prior to recruitment, the volunteers are called on to complete their labor service duty.

4. Prerequisites for recruitment are that the volunteer:
   a.) is a German citizen;
   b.) is worthy to bear arms;
   c.) is fit for service;
   d.) is not a Jew or a Jewish half-breed;
   e.) is fit to be a paratrooper on the strength of a military assessment;
   f.) is deemed fit to be a paratrooper after undergoing a psychological aptitude test;
   g.) has no prior convictions;
   h.) is not married; and
   i.) promises that he will support the National Socialist State unreservedly at all times.

The following documents are to be submitted by each applicant:
   a.) a handwritten curriculum vitae;
   b.) a certified declaration of consent from a legal relative;
   c.) Two passport photographs in civilian clothing without any head coverings; and
   d.) A certificate of voluntary entry (in the case of those who have already been registered, an excerpt from your service record book).

The curriculum vitae must contain the following details: date of birth; school attendance; occupation; sporting activity; and affiliation, where necessary, to an NSDAP (NS German Workers' Party – Nazi Party) division.

Application deadline:

1. For members of the agricultural population (provided your labor service duty is not yet sufficient), on 1 May of the previous year; and

2. For all other volunteers, on 1 October of the previous year.

3. Recruitment applications to be submitted to:

Fallschirm-Jäger-Rgt.1, Stendal/Altmark, Division: Recruitment.

(Early recruitment leaflet, original in Fallschirmjäger archives, held at Freiburg)

There is a propaganda film still in existence, produced by the *Wehrmacht* (armed forces) public relations machine, which depicts

Two stamps celebrating the exploits of the Fallschirmjäger, issued in 1943. Courtesy Lebrecht v. Blücher.

the training of the *Fallschirmjäger* troops. It is very professionally made and goes into considerable detail in showing the various aspects of the training regime experienced by recruits. The tone is decidedly heroic and the camera angles and lighting dramatic, but there is no doubting the rigor and attention to detail of the training. The film ends with a company of proudly swaggering *Fallschirmjäger* marching in formation from an aircraft hangar, wearing helmets, jump boots and smocks, singing their marching song, "*Rot scheint die Sonne.*" It is a stirring conclusion and one can readily imagine that German audiences watching the film in cinemas in 1940 would have believed these men to be true supermen. While the patriotic sound-track supports this impression, what is interesting in the film itself is the lack of fanaticism evident in the men themselves. They appear utterly dedicated to their profession and there is a great deal of camaraderie shown, but the overall impression is that these are extremely able soldiers, no doubt believing totally in their ability and skills, but men who retain the right to act on their own initiative. Undoubtedly the film was intended to bolster civilian morale and illustrate the superiority of Aryan men, in the form of dedicated Nazi paratroopers. To some extent it does this and there is no doubt that a proportion of *Fallschirmjäger* were dedicated Nazis; but look more closely at the scenes of training and it soon becomes apparent that these men are, in fact, exactly what paratroopers everywhere are supposed to be: physically tough; superbly trained; very close-knit; agile and aggressive; able to operate without direct orders; extremely proud of themselves and their unit; and totally confident of their ability to carry out the mission, whatever it may be.

Operations conducted at the beginning of the war, such as the assault on the Belgian fortress of Eben Emael, the taking of Norwegian airfields and the Dordrecht bridges in Holland reinforced the value of these qualities and provided dramatic proof of the validity of German doctrine for airborne troops (although heavy casualties and aircraft losses in some operations should have alerted planners to inherent weaknesses in German paratroop doctrine). Later, apart from rare raids such as that to rescue Benito Mussolini in 1944 and a drop behind enemy lines during the Battle of the Bulge also in 1944 the *Fallschirmjäger* were confined to mostly infantry roles. But their fighting spirit and skills in battle were shown again and again, from North Africa, to Italy, to Carentan in Normandy, to Arnhem and on the Eastern Front. As the war progressed the fighting qualities of the *Fallschirmjäger* allowed them to transform to the role of quick response shock troops, able to move rapidly to trouble spots and immediately go into action, usually stopping or at least delaying potentially disastrous enemy advances. Wherever they fought they earned the respect, indeed the admiration of their opponents. It is not without sound reasons that most airborne units around the world can trace the origins of their training regimes and unit ethos to the *Fallschirmjäger* of the 7th *Flieger* Division.

Surprisingly perhaps, the Germans were not the first to experiment with delivering troops to battle by aircraft and parachute. The Russians were conducting trials as early as 1928 and images of parachutists sliding off the broad wings of bomber aircraft illustrate the alarming nature and primitive techniques of those first paratroop maneuvers. While the delivery system was crude by standards adopted just a few years later, the Russians did develop what became the basic doctrine of parachute troops: they were to be essentially storm troops whose main task was to surprise the enemy by dropping behind enemy lines and capturing key facilities through quick, aggressive attacks. They would be lightly armed and required to hold captured positions until relieved by more heavily armed ground troops. Western observers first saw the potential for this type of soldiering in 1935,

Das Lied der Fallschirmjäger
Worte und Musik von Friedrich Schäfer

Rot scheint die Sonne, fertig gemacht,
wer weiß, ob sie morgen für uns auch noch lacht?
Werft an die Motoren, schiebt Vollgas hinein,
startet los, flieget an, heute geht es zum Feind!
In die Maschinen, in die Maschinen!

    Kamerad, da gibt es kein Zurück,
    fern im Westen
    stehen dunkle Wolken.
    komm mit und zage nicht, komm mit!

Donnern Motoren — Gedanken allein,
denkt jeder noch schnell an die Lieben daheim
Dann kommt, Kameraden, zum Sprung das Signal,
und wir schweben zum Feind, zünden dort das Fanal.
Schnell wird gelandet, schnell wird gelandet.

Klein unser Häuflein, wild unser Blut,
wir fürchten den Feind nicht und auch nicht den Tod.
Wir wissen nur eines, wenn Deutschland in Not,
zu kämpfen, zu siegen, zu sterben den Tod.
An die Gewehre, an die Gewehre.

A leaflet with the words to the Fallschirmjäger song, "Red Shines the Sun." Courtesy Fallschirmjäger archive, military archives, Freiburg.

when over one thousand Soviet paratroopers were dropped in one display. Realizing that he had witnessed a new and very promising method of attack, the German military attaché in the Soviet Union sent a report to Berlin which sparked the interest of staff officers who were then developing methods of combined arms operations in what became known as *Blitzkrieg* (lightning war) tactics. Ironically but not surprisingly in the Soviet Union of the 1930s, a purge of top Red Army officers included the commander-in-chief of the army, whose support had kept the parachute troop development going. With his demise went interest in the project and the idea of a Soviet operational airborne force languished for many years, though some small-scale operations were conducted by the Red Army during the Second World War.

In Berlin, Hermann Göring, command-in-chief of the *Luftwaffe* had been briefed on the Soviet developments and quickly ordered the formation of an experimental parachute battalion, drawn entirely from volunteers from the "General Göring" *Luftwaffe* Regiment. He would have been lobbied and briefed by Kurt Student, like himself a veteran of First World War flying. Göring would not be the last Nazi leader to succumb to Student's powers of persuasion and his complete confidence in both the correctness of his theories and the skills of his men. At the same time the German army was also developing a parachute unit, but their doctrine emphasized traditional infantry tactics rather than the more dramatic but riskier ideas being pursued in the *Luftwaffe*. In an effort to disguise from foreign observers the fact such a unit was being trained, the *Luftwaffe* designated the paratroopers as the 7th *Flieger* Division, a name which continued long after the Allies had come face to face with the division's troops.

In October 1935 the first batch of volunteers assembled at the Stendal base that was to become the main training establishment for parachute troops. Their entry into the First Parachute Regiment (the first battalion of which was formally "baptized" on 29 January 1936) was no easy task in itself, as the information sheet for prospective volunteers (reproduced above) makes clear. Psychological assessment and constant observation and evaluation while training helped to ensure that only the most able would graduate from the course. Two *Luftwaffe* officers instructed the men in parachute techniques and the three months training course was devised, developed and continuously refined by Major Bassenge. These first volunteers were required to meet high entry standards and this ensured that the emphasis would be on quality rather than quantity. While standards were lowered as the war went against Germany and the Eastern Front consumed ever increasing numbers of men, this rule, quality not quantity, was insisted upon through most of the war. Quite apart from the training received, this principle was responsible more than any other single factor for the consistency of the *Fallschirmjägers'* fighting prowess. They were simply better than average individuals who made great soldiers.

By the time *Graf* Wolfgang von Blücher began his training in 1940 the *Heer* (army) paratroop detachment had been integrated into the *Luftwaffe* paratroop regiment. General Student took command of the 7th

General Kurt Student, the guiding force and "father" of his beloved Fallschirmjäger. Bundesarchiv.

Parachute packing at Stendal. Courtesy Moog Collection.

Fallschirmjäger during training. Courtesy Moog Collection.

Practice parachute drop. Note the headfirst aircraft exit technique which was dictated by the design of the parachute. Courtesy Moog Collection.

Wolfgang's Wehrpass, issued when he first joined the army reserve.

Flieger Division in 1938 and by 1939, with the inclusion of the army paratroopers, a third battalion had been raised and the 2nd *Fallschirmjäger* Regiment formed. Student disagreed with the original "destroyer" small unit tactics envisaged for the paratroops. He felt that men in small units would stand little chance of survival; instead he developed a doctrine that had as its foundation the idea that paratroops would provide a decisive force in a battle. For the men who were to fight on Crete, this change of emphasis was to have severe implications, as it brought paratroops from a limited sphere of operations – operating as special forces behind enemy lines – to being a force which would be theoretically capable of mounting a large-scale assault against a well-entrenched enemy. Unfortunately, early actions in the war were more of the *coup de main* type and Student's doctrine was not properly tested until Operation Mercury.

The training that Wolfgang underwent was by 1940 well established. Men who met the requirements laid out on the information sheet were then given tests to weed out those prone to dizziness and airsickness. Those with a fear of heights were identified and dismissed after a drop from a fifteen-meter high tower into a tank of water. Less formal observation during this initial testing phase also determined suitability on the basis of physical and mental stamina. If all of these criteria were met, in addition to others on the recruiting leaflet list, trainees began an eight-week training course. There were exceptions granted to some of the criteria, an obviously greater than eighty-five kilogram former world heavyweight boxing champion Max Schmeling (who took part in the Crete assault) being a prominent example, but it would be no exaggeration to say that the men who were finally selected to begin *Fallschirmjäger* training were among the very best in the German Armed Forces. And, as the von Blücher brothers demonstrate, aristocratic family background did not guarantee any special treatment or automatic promotion to officer rank.

The training program was heavy on physical fitness, though this was always a means to a greater end. Every bit as important was developing in each man the confidence and skills to work both individually and as part of a team. In fact, along with an aggressive spirit and an unwavering determination to succeed, the ability to work with others as part of a team was a prized attribute. In both officers and enlisted men, these qualities were held above all. Officers underwent exactly the same training as enlisted men and they had to prove their worth in front of the men they would lead. As the grueling program progressed the bonds among the men grew ever stronger and their confidence in each other grew accordingly. Many armed forces use humiliation and the "break men to rebuild them" principle as the basic philosophy behind their recruit training. While the *Fallschirmjäger* course was no walk in the park and instructors were certainly demanding and uncompromising, breaking men down was never an aim of the two months course. On the contrary, all ranks were encouraged to be leaders, whether or not they actually held rank. This was perhaps a recognition that heavy casualties could be expected and a man may have to assume command in the middle of a battle with no prior notice. Leadership qualities were constantly being assessed during training, in addition to the more traditional skills in weapons handling, fieldcraft, tactics and such subjects as Nazi doctrine and military law. All trainees were interviewed at regular intervals by their commanding officer, who would provide each man with an evaluation of his progress which included a frank discussion of his strengths and weaknesses.

As the training progressed a strong camaraderie developed among the men. To some degree, this spirit was a continuation of what they had all experienced as members of the Hitler Youth. There was much of benefit to the armed forces to be found in a youth organization with shared beliefs, tests of self-confidence and initiative, basic military training and immersion in Nazi doctrine; all of these were part of a German boy's education in the 1930s. Camaraderie and its close relation *esprit de corps* are highly valued in many military forces and they are certainly not virtues found only among the *Fallschirmjäger*. But it seems that there was something special about these men. Perhaps it was the strong mutual regard held among

Hauling in the parachute after a training jump at Stendal.
Courtesy Moog Collection.

Part Two - The Making of the Fallschirmjäger

A well-composed shot taken during a training exercise. Courtesy Moog Collection.

officers and men; or the fighting spirit of the senior officers; or the quality of the training; or an unfailing belief in themselves and their comrades; or a mixture of these and other factors. What is clearly evident in every battle and campaign fought by the *Fallschirmjäger* is their ability to fight any opponent to a standstill and in many cases to prevail, whatever the odds. This standard of performance in battle existed even at the end of the war, when few new recruits had actually undergone parachute training and recruitment standards had been relaxed.

After two months of ground training, the sixteen days parachute course began. As would be the case in the Allied airborne units, the emphasis was on reaching a very high degree of competence to ensure the safety of all unit members: a paratrooper who injured or killed himself during the drop was of no use to the unit. Every technique required for jumping from an aircraft was mastered in drills practiced on the ground until they became second nature. Unlike Allied parachute units, which employed specialist riggers to pack the 'chutes, every *Fallschirmjäger*, officer or enlisted man, was responsible for packing his own parachute, assisted by one comrade. This simple requirement built mutual trust and ensured that every man took responsibility for himself when he leapt headfirst from the aircraft. Every man was required to make six descents before the award of the highly prized *Fallschirmschützenabzeichen* (Parachutists' Badge). These jumps were

Another dramatically composed photo of a training jump. Courtesy Moog Collection.

The highly prized Fallschirmjäger parachute qualification badge. Author photo.

made from different heights and one was made in poor visibility. Once qualified, the men were awarded their badges and took part in a passing-out parade that consisted of a march through the streets of Stendal. While this town remained the home of the *Fallschirmjäger*, other training schools were opened at Braunschweig and Wittstock.

The parachute itself was less than ideal. While parachutes similar to those used by Allied forces were already in use by *Luftwaffe* pilots, a less satisfactory model was chosen for the paratroops. This was because *Fallschirmjäger* doctrine decreed that jumps were to be made at 120 meters to reduce the amount of time men were in the highly vulnerable descent phase. Regular *Luftwaffe* parachutes were deemed unsuitable for this requirement. The RZ1 parachute (and later RZ16 and RZ20) did not allow for any maneuvering during descent as the straps were attached at the back rather than the shoulders. As well as the headfirst, spread-eagle dive from the plane to release the static line, the position of the straps on a man's back meant that landings were usually on all fours. This technique required men to wear special knee protectors and gloves, much like those still worn by many armed services today. Reserve parachutes were not carried. Other equipment unique to paratroopers was developed. The steel helmet was without the familiar neck guards of the German infantry helmet and its lining included rubber shock absorbers, a specially designed leather lining and a more supportive chinstrap. Despite losing some steel, this helmet was actually heavier than the standard infantry helmet. The original blue-grey paint was found to be reflective in the field and a variety of cloth covers was developed for operational use. A standard *Luftwaffe* blouse and trousers (similar to ski pants) uniform was worn on most occasions (much to the discomfort of the men who jumped on Crete in early summer heat). The boots were rubber soled, shin high and laced along the side of the boot, on the theory that this arrangement provided greater support and stability. This awkward design was soon replaced by a more conventional front-lacing system, though photographs taken on Crete show both designs in service. Covering the uniform to the lower thigh was a gabardine, olive green jump smock, early versions of which required the wearer to climb into and out of. This proved to be entirely impractical and the later versions were more like long jackets; later in the war these were made of camouflage material. Allied forces adopted similar smocks and in some cases nearly identically shaped helmets. In a role-specific right-hand trouser pocket, each paratrooper carried a knife for releasing fouled shrouds or cutting straps in the event of a tree or water landing. Cleverly designed, the knives could be opened with one hand and the blade dropped open (hence the "gravity knife" name given to them by collectors) and secured quickly by a thumb catch. Many men also wore red, heavily embroidered silk scarves or neckerchiefs underneath their smocks. Unlike their Allied counterparts, *Fallschirmjäger* carried little equipment on their persons, relying instead on being able to quickly access weapons and equipment containers which were dropped with the men. This approach would prove to be fatal to many men who found themselves stranded in open ground and unable to get to rifles (the standard German infantry Kar.98k) and machine guns. For their immediate protection after landing, every man wore a holstered semi-automatic pistol and had several grenades wedged into his leather waistbelt. Relatively few men, usually officers and senior NCOs, carried MP-40 sub-machine guns, thus rendering just-landed troops extremely vulnerable to a well-armed enemy.

Other equipment carried was minimal. Hanging from the waistbelt would have been a water-bottle with attached cup, mess tin, *Zeltban* (tent half shelter), a bayonet, perhaps a leather map-case for NCOs and officers, field glasses and MP-40 magazine pouches. Personal gear and light rations were carried in the traditional German soldier's canvas bread bag and the pockets of the jump smock. Total weight was a critical factor in ensuring a safe landing from a low-level drop and the weight restrictions were firmly enforced.

While the parachute may not have been ideal, the aircraft used for paratroop operations earned the trust and admiration of the men who jumped from it. The Junkers Ju 52 was already a veteran of civilian air transport routes by 1939, but it proved also to be a reliable, tough and

Men of the 2nd Battalion, 1st Fallschirmjäger Regiment before a training jump at Braunschweig-Broitzen in 1940. Courtesy Fallschirmjäger archive, military archives, Freiburg.

stable platform for airborne operations. Various versions of the three-engined Ju 52 could carry between twelve and seventeen men, with the jumps being made through the side fuselage door. The men sat on benches along the sides of the plane and while they had great faith in *"Tante Ju,"* they endured noisy, uninsulated cabins sitting on cold metal or wood seats, often at turbulent low altitudes. Normal procedure was for the pilot to reduce speed from the usual 250kph cruise to around 180kph for parachute drops. In combat and under fire this ideal drop speed was rarely achieved and in practice, combat jumps were made at higher speeds.

In the unlikely event that a paratrooper needed reminding of his elite status, a reading of a small label sewn inside his pack would refresh his memory. Reputedly written by Hitler himself but more likely from Kurt Student's pen, the *Fallschirmjäger's Ten Commandments* gave a no-nonsense summary of what it meant to wear that handsome badge on the left breast.

The Fallschirmjäger's Ten Commandments

1. You are the elite of the *Wehrmacht*. For you, combat shall be fulfillment. You shall seek it out and train yourself to stand any test.

2. Cultivate true comradeship, for together with your comrades you will triumph or die.

Paratroopers training with a mortar. Courtesy Moog Collection.

3. Be shy of speech and incorruptible. Men act, women chatter; chatter will bring you to your grave.

4. Calm and caution, vigor and determination, valor and a fanatical offensive spirit will make you superior in attack.

5. In facing the foe, ammunition is the most precious thing. He who shoots uselessly, merely to reassure himself, is a man without guts. He is a weakling and does not deserve the title of paratrooper.

6. Never surrender. Your honor lies in Victory or Death.

7. Only with good weapons can you have success. So look after them on the principle: first my weapons, then myself.

8. You must grasp the full meaning of an operation so that, should your leader fall by the way, you can carry it out with coolness and caution.

9. Fight chivalrously against an honest foe; armed irregulars deserve no quarter.

10. Keep your eyes wide open. Tune yourself to the top-most pitch. Be nimble as a greyhound as tough as leather, as hard as Krupp steel and so you will be the German warrior incarnate.

The training was excellent and the quality of the men first-rate. But the real test of just how good the *Fallschirmjäger* was would be the first operational jumps. Once the war began, the operations were not long in coming.

Within two months of the outbreak of war on 3rd September 1939 planning was

A training jump. Note the low altitude of the drop. Courtesy Moog Collection.

underway for the assault on the Belgian fortress of Eben Emael and the bridges over the Albert canal. This dramatic, bold and astonishingly successful operation immediately gave the *Fallschirmjäger* hero status in Germany. While it was a small unit assault, it appeared to vindicate Student's theories and silenced more conservative critics of airborne assaults. In April 1940 paratroopers took airfields and bridges in Denmark, as well as airfields in Norway. For Wolfgang's part in the Oslo and Narvik assaults he was awarded the Iron Cross, First and Second Class. The next month he took part in the invasion of the Netherlands and for leadership and courage during the assault on the Dordrecht bridges he received the Knight's Cross. During the same month the glider assault on the Eben Emael fortress demonstrated both the élan and skill of the participating troops and the worth of paratroops in surprise assaults that made use of imaginative and daring tactics. All of these operations were successful, some spectacularly so, but the circumstances were very different from those to be faced on Crete. There was no doubt that against a weak and ill-equipped foe, a well planned and executed parachute assault could be decisive. The great danger lay in assuming that future operations would be just as successful, despite very different operational conditions in almost every respect.

One of a series of postcards depicting Fallschirmjäger Knight's Cross winners in heroic action poses. Courtesy Lebrecht v. Blücher.

Part Three
The Knight's Cross

The German plan for the conquest of the Low Countries included the possibility that the Netherlands might surrender without a fight. In the event that the Dutch did decide to defend their country, German plans for a quick victory included the first substantial use of airborne troops, both parachutists and air-landing units, to capture the seat of government and secure key airfields and bridges. As the Germans had hopes for a Dutch capitulation without a fight, few units were allocated and hence available for an invasion. Even the 1st FJR (*Fallschirmjäger* Regiment) was not at full strength. Had the Dutch succeeded in stopping both ground and mechanized units advancing from the south, the paratroops tasked with taking The Hague and important bridges would have had to hold their positions for longer than planned. The Germans were gambling on overwhelming any Dutch resistance before it could be properly organized, despite the fact that aerial reconnaissance showed the movement of troops to areas around airfields and bridges in anticipation of airborne assaults. The Dutch had watched German progress in Denmark and Norway and noted the use of paratroops to take airfields in those countries. Unfortunately for the Dutch, the troops positioned at airfields and bridges were poorly trained and equipped. In the event, the plan to take The Hague and capture the royal family and government failed to make quick progress; this necessitated implementation of the back-up plan: to take the bridges at Rotterdam, Dordrecht and Moerdijk and thus permit the fast deployment north of mechanized forces.

Two bridges alongside each other, one railway and the other for road traffic, connect the islands of Dordrecht and Ysselmonde. They cross the Oude Maas and are situated between the cities of Dordrecht and Zwijndrecht, located to the south of Rotterdam.

The first battalion (less one company, which had been badly mauled in Norway) of 1st FJR was assigned to take the twin bridges, form a strong bridgehead to defend against counterattacks and gain control of the city of Dordrecht and a nearby motorway. Tactically, the bridges and their surroundings presented the attackers with problems: the paratroops would have to cross open ground to reach the bridges and strong concrete structures gave the defenders plenty of cover. The battle that followed the landings should have given the commander of 1FJRI (First Battalion of the First *Fallschirmjäger* Regiment) pause

A paratrooper in action during the invasion of Holland in May 1940. Courtesy Moog Collection.

for thought as he prepared for the Crete operation. While German propaganda had portrayed the invasion of the Netherlands as a pushover, there were, in fact, some very nasty moments. At Dordrecht the Dutch put up some determined resistance and in so doing highlighted some severe weaknesses in German paratroop doctrine. Most significant for the Crete operation was the difficulty men had in reaching weapons containers after landing. Many paratroopers were shot down as they raced across open land in an effort to get to machine-guns and rifles. Secondly, the physical landscape, with its many polders (low-lying areas of land, reclaimed from marshes or the sea and surrounded by embankments) made large-scale drops difficult. The resulting inability to quickly assemble a large enough force to bring about a decisive victory meant that the smaller company and platoon size groups were vulnerable to a determined counter-attack. Despite achieving initial surprise some small groups of the *Fallschirmjäger* took heavy casualties as they found themselves on exposed ground and without heavy weapons. Strong leadership and some daring and courageous small unit actions eventually secured the bridges, but not without much heavier losses than had been expected.

Oberst Bruno Bräuer, who commanded the 1st *Fallschirmjäger* Regiment, was already a legendary figure among his men. Never without his gold cigarette case and always close to the action, Bräuer had been awarded the Iron Cross First and Second Class during the First World War. After

May 1940: paratroopers at a road junction in Holland. Note the road sign at extreme right pointing to Dordrecht. Courtesy Moog Collection.

the war he joined the *Reichswehr* (the post-World War I and pre-Nazi era army) and eventually became commanding officer of the Hermann Göring Regiment. In 1936 he had the distinction of being the first German paratrooper to jump from an aircraft and in 1938 he took command of the 1st Battalion of the 1st *Fallschirmjäger* Regiment (1FJRI). He was a "press on regardless" style of leader, greatly respected by those who served with him. For his leadership and personal bravery during the Dordrecht operation he was awarded the Knight's Cross. *General der Flieger* Kurt Student described him succinctly and vividly: "He was a complex and prickly personality, a real man who feared neither death nor the devil. He was courageous, upright and straight, proper and faultless. As he behaved throughout his life, he also met his death." (*quoted in Bräuer's biographical entry at www.ritterkreuzträger-1939-1945.com*). He was to figure prominently in the fate of *Graf* Wolfgang and *Graf* Hans Joachim von Blücher on Crete. At least some aspects of Bräuer's personality, as described by Kurt Student, could be applied to Wolfgang and Bräuer must have been aware of the daring and leadership skills displayed by the young *Leutnant* at Dordrecht; and of the way in which his eight man action led to a decisive victory. This was the sort of officer who took after Bruno Bräuer's own heart and who could be relied upon to carry out the most demanding tasks.

1FJRI veteran Gerhard Broder recalled his first meeting with Wolfgang when the latter became his platoon leader. "He has

Oberst Bruno Bräuer, the other "Father of the Fallschirmjäger," in a portrait painted by Willrich for a 1940 postcard series. Author's collection.

a formal bearing and wears his officer's cap off to one side at a jaunty angle. *Graf* von Blücher finds personal satisfaction in high sporting achievements. On duty and in battle he does not merely order his men; rather he inspires individual soldiers and groups into attacking. He is a charismatic leader. He takes condescending remarks about the aristocrat in his stride. He has a reserved friendliness." (*La Guerre Mondiale Contre Moi*, Gerhard Broder, p.17)

Shortly before 05:00 on 10 May the 3rd company of the 1st battalion landed in "*De Polder*," to the south of Dordrecht. One platoon dropped almost on top of the road bridge and despite the difficult open approaches and well-protected Dutch troops, the initial assault by Wolfgang's company on the lightly defended road bridge achieved surprise and the few Dutch troops on guard duty were quickly disposed of. Other platoons of the 3rd company,

Paratroopers relax after their hard-fought victory at Dordrecht. Courtesy Moog Collection.

which landed further south of Dordrecht did not meet with such immediate success. In nearby Dordrecht were some 1,500 Dutch army pioneers (combat engineers). Many were barely out of recruit training and they were lightly armed. However, unsuitable terrain meant that not all German troops could be landed directly on or alongside the bridges. While the road bridge had been quickly secured, other platoons came under some determined Dutch resistance. The Dutch troops had been quick to reorganize after the initial shock of the landings and they now began systematic patrolling which destroyed German machine-gun positions. Once these vital defensive positions were taken, the Dutch gradually closed in around the German positions. After some fierce skirmishes and the loss of their company commander, the paratroops found themselves being surrounded and were eventually overrun by the Dutch.

Some eighty members of the 3rd company were taken prisoner and fourteen were killed. By this point in the battle 1FJRI had been reduced to little more than two companies. Nonetheless, the paratroopers were able to successfully defend the bridges against two counter-attacks.

Despite a confused drop which saw one platoon land over The Hague and others a long way from their objective (some enterprising troops chartered a bus to drive them to their proper objective), *Oberst* Bräuer, the regimental commander, was quickly informed of the loss of his 3rd company and immediately ordered his two remaining companies to advance towards the southwest approach to Dordrecht. This force made rapid progress, but when they approached the town they came under fire from the direction of the Dutch headquarters. To defeat this pocket of resistance a plan was rapidly devised: a heavy machine gun

German paratroopers escort captured Dutch troops after their surrender. Courtesy Moog Collection.

Following their daring assault, Wolfgang (on the right, wearing a peaked cap) and his men inspect the Dutch command bunker they captured at Dordrecht. (Biblio-Verlag, Bissendorf)

platoon would advance along the motorway to distract the defenders and a smaller unit, under the command of *Leutnant* Wolfgang *Graf* von Blücher, was ordered to take the Dutch position by surprise assault.

Wolfgang reconnoitered the area and decided to take his squad of seven men across a wide waterway and attack from the west. He found a suitable place to swim across and led his men through a park to the outskirts of the Dutch positions. Then, armed only with pistols, grenades and several rifles, Wolfgang and his squad rushed the Dutch, hurling grenades and screaming at the tops of their voices. The seventy-five Dutch defenders, taken utterly by surprise and panic-stricken hid in any available cover while Wolfgang's men continued to plaster the position with their grenades and pistol fire. Many of the Dutch had taken cover inside two large concrete bunkers and most of those inside were killed when German grenades were dropped into the bunkers' observation slits. Taking advantage of the confused Dutch situation and a commander rendered temporarily unconscious by a grenade blast, the German heavy machine gun platoon then quickly took the entire Dutch position. Within minutes the Dutch headquarters was out of action and its surviving members had surrendered. Twenty-five Dutch soldiers had been killed against five Germans. Wolfgang had been grazed on the face by a bullet, but his leadership, tactical skill and personal courage had ensured victory. He and his seven men had defeated a force of seventy-five. Wolfgang and his men had carried out a classic small unit action, but one which was decisive in that it took out of action the senior leadership of the Dutch forces.

The railway bridge, which on account of its construction favored the defenders, was taken only after heavy German losses. Many of these were the result of the mistaken German belief that the Dutch had retreated from their positions on and near the bridge. German troops marched in formation across the bridge, only to be met with fierce machine-gun fire, causing confusion and casualties. However, superior German firepower was brought to bear on the defenders and the Dutch commanders quickly realized the futility of further resistance. Nevertheless, some Dutch positions near the bridge continued to hold out and in fact threatened the security of the German bridgehead. To defeat this bar to progress, Bräuer requested reinforcements and the arrival of additional forces relieved the immediate threat, though the situation remained in stalemate for several days.

The city of Dordrecht and its bridges were finally secured after the arrival of tanks of the 9th *Panzer* Division fought a costly battle against some strong Dutch resistance. The German airborne forces involved in the fighting in the Netherlands suffered heavy casualties – the 22nd *Luftlande-Division* lost 40% of its officers and 28% of other ranks (figures quoted in Kurowski, p.53, *op.cit.*) – and nearly 200 Ju 52 transport aircraft had been destroyed. At Dordrecht, nearly a third of the airborne force had been killed, wounded or captured. While the performance overall of the airborne forces reinforced their tactical significance and their individual fighting prowess, the battle for the Dordrecht was by no means an easy victory. It is remarkable

Wolfgang after the award of his Knight's Cross in May 1940. Courtesy Gertrud v. Ketelhodt.

Part Three - The Knight's Cross

In photos taken after the invasion of Holland, in which Wolfgang was awarded the Knight's Cross (note that he is wearing all his decorations), he is shown leading his men on an exercise. Courtesy Yannis Prekatsounakis.

that *Generalleutnant* Student, who was severely wounded in the head at the end of the fighting in Holland by what is generally assumed to be friendly fire, and his staff did not adequately apply the lessons learned there to the planning for the Crete operation.

Following the Netherlands invasion and the award of his Knight's Cross, Wolfgang requested and was granted extended leave so that he could return to the family estates and manage them. While it may seem unusual to release from service a distinguished combat leader, Germany was enjoying a brief period during which it seemed that the war may soon be won and many servicemen were either granted leave or discharge after the campaign in Western Europe.

There was one further honor for Wolfgang after the Dordrecht action. He was recommended for promotion to *Oberleutnant* by his battalion commander, *Major* Erich Walther. The recommendation was seconded by regimental commander, *Oberst* Bräuer. *Major* Walther's comments on the young officer are very succinct, but the few words give an insight into how Wolfgang was perceived in his battalion and regiment:

> *Lt. Count von Blücher is fearless. His manner of leading is inspiring because of his dashing personal commitment. Any assignment can be confidently given to him. He has proven himself superbly several times as a leader of a raiding patrol during the actions fought by the battalion.*
>
> *Blücher is an intelligent and self-confident officer and an exemplary comrade as well. He has excellent relations with his subordinates and at the same time maintains the necessary distance. I would like to highlight especially his concern for the welfare of his troops. He himself lives sparingly and unpretentiously.*
>
> *Blücher has been awarded the Knight's Cross. He is unequivocally qualified for the advancement to a First Lieutenant.*

The original document from Wolfgang's personnel file (see illustration on page XXX) is marked with a cross and the word *Gefallen* (killed in action).

```
1. Fliegerdivision 7 Berlin          v. 31.7.40 of. 7.Kr.    L.P. 33700/40 g.
2. I./Fallschirm-Jäger Rgt.1 Stendal
3. W.B.K.: Schwerin (Meckl.)                                 Oblt. d.R.
4. Vorgeschlagen gem.: D.R.d.L.u.Ob.d.L. LP Az. B (21 o.10.10.
                       Nr.1886/6.40 (3 IA) v. 24.6.1940.

                            V o r s c h l a g .
                            ─────────────────────
              zur Beförderung des Leutnant d.R. Graf von Blücher
                         zum Oberleutnant d.R.

Vor u. Zuname:   Wolfgang Graf von Blücher
Geburtsdatum:    31.1.1917
Dienstgrad:      Leutnant d.R.
Rangdienstalter: 1.4.1938
5. Eingesetzt als: Zugführer
6. Geeignet zum:   Zugführer
Aktiver Wehrdienst seit: 21.1.1940
Teilnahme an welchen Kämpfen: Oslo(Süd-Norw.), Dortrecht, Eins.Narvik.
Wird vorgeschlagen zur Beförderung zum: Oberleutnant d.R.

Kurze Beurteilung durch den Rgt. Kdr., selbst.Btl.-usw.Kdr. hin-
sichtlich dienstlicher Leistung, Führerpersönlichkeit und Stellung
im Kameradenkreis:

Lt. Graf von Blücher ist ein Draufgänger. Seine Führung ist durch
schneidigen persönlichen Einsatz mitreißend. Ihm kann jede Aufgabe
anvertraut werden. Er hat sich bei den Gefechten des Btl. als
Stoßtruppführer mehrfach hervorragend bewährt.
Blücher ist ein intelligenter und selbstbewußter Offizier und zu-
gleich ein vorbildlicher Kamerad. Zu seinen Untergebenen hat er
unter Wahrung des erforderlichen Abstandes das denkbar beste Ver-
hältnis. Die Fürsorge für die Truppe ist besonders hervorzuheben.
Er selbst lebt sparsam und anspruchslos.
Blücher ist Träger des Ritterkreuzes. Er ist zur Beförderung zum
Oberleutnant d.R. uneingeschränkt geeignet.

                                          Hauptmann und Btl.-Kdr.

Stellungnahme des Rgt.-Kdr.:
Einverstanden.

Oberst und Rgt.-Kdr.
```

Major Walther's recommendation for Wolfgang's promotion to Oberleutnant. Oberst Bräuer's signature is at bottom left. This document, from Wolfgang's service record, notes the date of his death in action by the handwritten note at upper left and the cross on the page. Courtesy Fallschirmjäger archive, military archives, Freiburg.

The handmade leather cover for Wolfgang's Knight's Cross award certificate. Courtesy Andreas Thies.

Wolfgang's Knight's Cross award certificate, signed by Adolf Hitler.
Courtesy Andreas Thies.

Part Four
Crete

Once Mussolini's botched invasion of Greece had been successfully concluded by German forces, Crete became an important island for both sides. British, Commonwealth and Greek forces had been sent there ahead of the German conquest of the Greece and additional troops escaped to the island before they could fall into German hands on the mainland. Crete's airfields and ports held strategic value to both Germany and Britain. For the Germans, Crete represented a base from which the *Luftwaffe* could raid British installations in Egypt and protect the increasingly important (given the impending invasion of the Soviet Union) oilfields in Romania. In addition, the fact that the remnants of the defeated British forces in Greece were on Crete offered an opportunity to complete in detail what had already been another sweeping victory for the *Wehrmacht*. Above all, both sides saw Crete as the key to dominance in the Eastern Mediterranean; whoever had the airfields and harbors could control the entire area.

So a German invasion of Crete and British determination to hold onto it were never in doubt. The problem from the German side was British naval domination of the Mediterranean. The strength of the Royal Navy and a lack of suitable landing ships precluded a seaborne assault on Crete. For General Kurt Student, these obstacles represented an opportunity for him to prove the strategic worth of his *Fallschirmjäger*. The island was only 300 kilometers from the Greek mainland, which would allow for maximum air support and the three main airfields on Crete presented both excellent targets and ready-made entry points for a quick build-up of troops once the paratroops had secured the airports and major towns. Of course, all of these factors were equally well known to the British, whose planning for the defense of Crete assumed an attack similar to what Student had in mind. Beyond tactical considerations, Crete's geography meant that an attack on the southern side of the island was virtually out of the question: even if an invading force had been able to land at the few suitable areas, rugged mountain ranges would have stood between them and the real prizes, the airfields and ports on the northern coast.

Then there was ULTRA. General Bernard Freyberg VC, the New Zealand general in command of the defense of Crete, was supplied with decrypts of German orders and signals relating to Crete soon after they were sent to their intended recipients. The knowledge he gained from the German signals allowed him to position his forces for maximum defensive effect and to construct formidable positions around the proposed German objectives. And while British intelligence was accurate and plentiful, Student would be very badly let down by his own. It consistently and grossly underestimated Allied strength on Crete and misled Student as to the fighting ability of the various British, Commonwealth and Greek units and to the attitude of Cretans towards a German invasion. As if this were not enough, the usually thorough German staff work and planning were deficient in some key areas, partly through reliance on the poor intelligence estimates and partly the result of the fact that the operation, named "*Merkur*" or Mercury, was so hastily conceived. Adolf Hitler, then at his peak as a military leader, delayed giving the go-ahead, having expressed great skepticism about the operation and fearing heavy casualties; but he was eventually won over by the very persuasive Kurt Student, now commanding the XI. *Flieger-Korps*, who could point to the spectacular paratroop operations of 1940 in supporting his case. Perhaps Hitler's focus was on a much larger up-coming Operation "Barbarossa," the invasion of the Soviet Union, which was to begin less than two months after Crete had been taken. Operation *Merkur* was approved on 25 April 1941, less than a month before its launch

Detailed planning began immediately and the first logistical challenge (complicated by the fact that preparations for Barbarossa were not to be disrupted by requirements for Mercury) was to transport some 6,000 paratroops and 750 glider-borne troops from Germany to Greece in secret. As the von Blücher brothers were hurriedly assembled with their units at their bases at Stendal and Tangermünde (Lebrecht), they and their comrades would have sensed that this would be more than just a surgical drop on top of a fortress. The Greek campaign had been reported in detail in the nation's media and while the target was secret, many men must have guessed that they were headed to the Mediterranean.

Student devised a plan that was complex in its detail but perfectly simple in its conception; in fact, there were few options. His decision to assault all three airfields on the north coast – Maleme, Rethymnon and Heraklion – almost simultaneously was ambitious, in that it would require massive numbers of Ju 52s, gliders and supporting bombers. A number of poorly prepared airfields near Athens, with grass runways and unreliable communications with Athens and each other would also have to be pressed into use, despite their obvious deficiencies. The three-pronged plan also meant that his paratroop force would be divided into three, thus dispersing his lightly armed forces instead of focusing the effort against one major target. From the beginning, overconfidence blighted German planning, encouraged by hopelessly inadequate intelligence reports. There were warning signals in the form of objections raised by *Luftwaffe* planners. Their concerns, such as the potential for delayed and confused air operations and their consequences for landings and ground combat, were countered by *Fallschirmjäger* leaders who had experienced only successes and now had a chance to demonstrate that their regiments were capable of large-scale, decisive operations as well as the small-

Temporary airfield at Tanagra, Greece, prior to the Crete operation.
Courtesy Moog Collection.

Ju 52 pilots relax at their Greek airfield in late April 1941, just before the start of Operation Merkur. Courtesy Moog Collection.

Wearing their distinctive red scarves, Fallschirmjäger pass the time at their airfield before the flight to Crete. Courtesy Moog Collection.

scale spectaculars. These men had been in command when their units suffered heavy casualties in Norway and Holland; and they had seen the vulnerability of the low-flying and slow Ju 52s to concentrated ground fire; now, in their enthusiasm to prove once and for all the worth of their form of warfare, such lessons were put to one side. And after all, what could 5,000 British and assorted Commonwealth troops who had been chased down through Greece and off the mainland do against some of the best troops in the *Wehrmacht*? Rather like the Allied planners in the Pacific and European campaigns, much faith was placed in the ability of air bombing to reduce defenses to rubble so that, in theory at least, when the troops arrived there would be little to do but clean up. In hindsight, errors such as this and overconfidence based on earlier, but dissimilar operations are difficult to understand. At the time, however, Student had no reason to doubt the efficiency of the German intelligence organization, or in the ability of the *Luftwaffe* to mount a complex bombing and troop-delivery operation; perhaps most of all he had complete confidence in his men, who had proven themselves in every fight they had been in. Veterans like Wolfgang von Blücher may have realized that this was going to be a very different battle from those they had experienced in Norway and Holland, but for inexperienced youngsters like Lebrecht and Hans Joachim (according to his sister Gertrud, so condensed had his training been that his first and only parachute jump was the one he made at Heraklion), there must have been great excitement, mixed with apprehension of course, as they were briefed about this assault on an island which was best known for its ancient Minoan civilization and associated myths. It must have seemed the beginning of a great adventure, so much more exciting than boarding school at Misdroy.

A group of Fallschirmjäger examining a map before the Crete operation. Note the elaborate embroidery on the scarf worn by the man at center. Courtesy Moog Collection.

What Student did not know, of course, was that the Allied troops on Crete had been reinforced from Egypt and now numbered some 42,000, of whom about half were trained and equipped to fight as organized infantry. Nor was he aware that the Allied commanders on Crete were receiving frequent summaries of intercepted German plans. Finally, Student would have been very surprised to have learned that the Allies were busily preparing strong defensive positions around the three airfields on the island and that they were well equipped with anti-aircraft guns, field artillery and even light tanks. So while the paratroopers were being briefed on what looked like yet another easy victory, General Freyberg and his men were readying themselves with equal confidence. The British had been on Crete since October 1940 and they had immediately begun the construction of defensive works at strategic points around the airfields and the ports. The lightly-armed paratroopers would be easy prey for the strongly protected and heavily armed defenders.

As late as the 19th of May German intelligence was confirming that Allied forces on Crete numbered no more than 5,000. At the same time, the British commanders were receiving up to the minute reports of German preparations (though only General Freyberg and his closest staff knew the origin of these reports) and had completed the positioning of their men and equipment.

Martin Pöppel was an *Oberjäger* with a machine gun battalion and was to drop near Rethymnon. In his entertaining memoir he recalled the night of the 19th of May:

"That evening we gathered under a huge olive tree, drank beer and sang our

Men assemble for a pre-departure briefing, with some of their equipment in the foreground. Courtesy Moog Collection.

The eternal wait, familiar to all soldiers, with a map showing the Mediterranean area set up for a briefing. Courtesy Moog Collection.

songs accompanied by *Oberleutnant* Büttner's [company commander, killed on the 21st of May] band. Was it premonition that we didn't just sing cheerful soldiers' songs as usual, but also included nostalgic songs of home? For most men it would be the first parachute jump [in combat] and only a few – such as myself – knew what death in action was really like. Maybe many realized, even had a premonition, that lads, so fresh and young and full of optimism, were to fall in battle during the next few days." (Martin Pöppel, *Heaven and Hell: The War Diary of a German Paratrooper*, p.54)

Such informal gatherings would have been held at all the airfields and no doubt the von Blücher brothers also sang and drank with their comrades that night, sharing the strength to be gained from the camaraderie of fellow *Fallschirmjäger* while also reflecting privately on what the next day might bring.

On the eve of battle domestic chores still consume a man's attention. Note his distinctive first pattern jump boots, with the laces along the outer side of each boot. Courtesy Moog Collection.

Preparing a contents list for a container holding medical supplies. Its impact-absorbing container is clearly visible, as is the red cross mark for quick identification in the field. Courtesy Moog Collection.

Wolfgang wrote this letter home to his mother while travelling by train to Athens. It was posted on 19 May 1941, the day before the Crete invasion began and two days before Wolfgang's death. Courtesy Gertrud v. Ketelhodt.

Gerhard Broder remembers that on the day before the operation began he and his comrades relaxed by going for a swim in the nearby bay; later they bought a donkey for 20 Reichmarks and travelled on donkey-back to a mountain village where they enjoyed a mocha coffee. (Phone interview with G. Broder, by L. von Blücher, August 2012)

Wolfgang posted a final letter to his mother, written on the journey to Greece, but held for posting for security reasons until the operation had begun.

On the way in Hungary
L 33450, LGP. Vienna, May 5th 1941
[posted from Athens on 19 May 1941]

My beloved Mother,
I have to thank you for your letter of the 24th, which I received before our departure. At the moment we are in very good spirits. I know from last year the excitement of preparing for action, but you should see Lebs [Lebrecht] and Jochen [Hans Joachim]! Their delight in being soldiers is even stronger than previously.

However, I am only guessing about Lebs, because the last time I met him was in Tangermünde. I think I mentioned that to you already. It will probably be a long time before you receive this letter, because it will only be sent to you from the place where we leave for our mission. A year ago it was Dortmund! More than eight days ago we were ordered from Altengrabow ahead of schedule and we left Stendal on the morning of April 4th. Lebs had already left two days earlier.

Hatta [stepfather] phoned me at Stendal one or two days beforehand and learned that we are still there! I can imagine that you thought that we had arrived in Greece after listening to the special announcements on the radio. But unfortunately this is not the case. We strongly hope that our mission will come about and that we can push the Tommies [British troops] somewhere else.

I have been appointed transport commander. I have to command my 2nd company and half of the 1st company. That includes Jochen, too. It is so good to have him with me! Yesterday he paid me a visit in my compartment. He really presents himself excellently. If you say something to him he immediately understands. Both he and Lebs will soon jump for their first time and they will do so in the face of the enemy.

We will be happy to see you in Posen for the first time! When will that be? And what will we see and experience before then?! Up to this point the travel has been superb. It is a pity that we passed through Prague and Vienna in the dark. Yesterday evening we stopped a long way outside of Budapest, so we could see the town only in the distance. It is the second time that I have travelled into spring. It is so beautiful. We are approaching the Rumanian border. The lilacs are in full flower. The people cheer us in a very friendly way. We see old grandmothers coming out of their houses, climbing on the fences and waving to us with both arms.

At this station we have already been waiting for two hours. Just now I went to the village together with a comrade. I asked a German-speaking Hungarian if we could see some horses. Immediately they showed us the stables inside which were the best Hungarian horses. The people are very supportive of us and it seems to us that they are grateful to receive the regions back. They are very attached to their mother country. It hurts them to have lost the regions in 1918.

I received a letter from A. [brother Adolf] dated the 19th. He is well and it seems he has experienced a lot and he is enjoying his flying. That must indeed be a magnificent experience. As we draw closer to the start of our mission the long waiting time is quickly forgotten. I have asked Jochen to invite the wife of my boss, Mrs. Gröschke, [to Darze] as long as we are not in Stendal. Mrs Gröschke is very kind, however she is a real townswoman. Then Ichen [sister Elisabeth] will no longer be the only woman in Darze. I think in the long-term it will be boring for her. In addition Mrs. Gröschke will bring a maid with her so Ichen will have more time to ride and to do the garden.

Yes, it is permissible for you to send parcels for the youngsters to me. Jochen has asked me to forward parcels which are already on the way from Ichen and you [to Stendal] to his comrades from the school in Misdroy. I therefore have left their addresses in the office in Stendal in order that all arriving printed matter will be forwarded to them. At the moment

A briefing before the Crete operation. Courtesy Moog Collection.

it is very difficult. I cannot send home information, as I have a feeling that the mission might begin very soon. One has to obey the rules of secrecy. So I will end. A thousand best wishes to all of you and a big kiss for you,

Yours
Wolfe

The next morning, the 20th, at Topolia, 100 kilometers north of Athens, the men of the 1st Battalion, 1st Parachute Regiment had completed their briefings and were preparing themselves for the mission. Unseen by them, a massive air operation was also gearing up for action: some 600 Ju 52s; eighty gliders; air cover consisting of 280 bombers, including 150 Ju 87 Stukas; and 180 fighters to protect the bombers. Their flights had to be coordinated with the landing operations at Maleme, Galatas, Chania, Rethymnon and Heraklion. It was an immensely complex air operation that required precise timings for all the parachute drops and which could be undone by any one of many possible hitches. Most damaging to the overall operation, due to a shortage of transport aircraft, the paratroops could not be dropped in one mass assault wave, as per the original plan. As well as weakening the strength of the attacking

Boarding the Ju 52. The paratroopers' protective gloves and kneepads are clearly visible. Courtesy Moog Collection.

forces, the need to re-use aircraft created another set of potential problems: these related to aircraft losses on the first run; the need to refuel aircraft by hand pumps – a slow and cumbersome operation – because of a lack of modern facilities and trained ground crews at the temporary fields; any delays would also require the bombers and fighters to re-schedule their missions. Because of these limitations, the assault was broken into three groups dropping or landing in four sectors and in two waves. *Gruppe West* (Maleme) would drop at 07:15; *Gruppe Mitte* (Middle) (Chania) at 16:15 and *Gruppe Ost* (East) (Heraklion) at 15:15. As soon as the paratroops had secured the airfields, 14,000 ground troops, including specialist mountain units, would begin landing.

These concerns were far from the minds of the men of the First and Second Battalions. Take-off was scheduled for 13:00, with the first elements due to drop at 15:15. The early morning was spent preparing equipment, cleaning weapons and finding space in pockets for spare socks and pants (woolen, just like those worn in Norway and Denmark; captured British stores would provide the first tropical kit available to the men), a small *Esbit* solid fuel stove and two days rations (including a chocolate bar, cubes of bread, toilet paper, water purification tablets and a phonetic Greek phrase book), half a dozen grenades and whatever personal items could be crammed into pockets. Once everything had been cleaned and checked, it was re-checked; the men sat in tight groups, going over their orders and chatting, reassuring others while seeking reassurance from the company of comrades. For soldiers geared up, physically and mentally, for battle, long delays meant time to think about what lay ahead.

The first drops were by the Western and Centre groups. There was an element of surprise achieved in these early landings, as the British had understood that the landings would take place on 17 May. When these failed to occur the defending troops began to believe that perhaps the invasion would never happen, even as the daily bombing raids continued. However, surprise was quickly replaced by fierce reaction and both paratroopers and aircraft suffered heavy casualties. So began a chain reaction that reached back to the waiting men of *Gruppe Ost* and set in motion a series of delays which would have near disastrous consequences for them. At Topolia the heat on the airfield, where the troops were assembled without shelter, became intense by midday. As returning aircraft landed, some crash-landing due to damage from anti-aircraft fire, huge clouds of dust were raised, covering men and equipment. More dust clouds were raised as aircraft throttled up for take-off. It was then that the call went out for the troops to assist with re-fuelling. Ground crews were not available at Topolia and the paratroopers were inexperienced in handling the pumps and in the procedures for re-fuelling. The job required clambering on wings and the men had to quickly shed the encumbrance of all the carefully assembled parachute harnesses and equipment, much to their irritation. Scheduled departure time quickly passed as the runway was cleared of damaged planes, forcing returning aircraft to circle and delay landing. Even when the runway was cleared they had to wait until the dust stirred by other aircraft had settled.

Despite all the careful planning the timetable had become hopelessly compromised. Perhaps if the planners had had more time to consider all the possible ramifications of dusty airfields, unexpectedly heavy aircraft losses, time taken to refuel and the possibility that intelligence reports were inaccurate, then the next twenty four hours would have been very different for the men of the first and second battalions of the first regiment. As it was, 600 of the 2,300 men of the 1st *Fallschirmjäger* Regiment had to be left behind due to lack of aircraft. Overconfidence, poor intelligence regarding enemy dispositions and numbers, dispersal of forces thus weakening the assaults, troops too lightly armed … bravery alone cannot compensate for such failures.

A preliminary German after-action report on Operation Mercury described the situation faced by Bräuer and his men bluntly:

"GROUP EAST

"A prerequisite for the success of the attack was the dropping of all parachute units over their objective areas at 15:15, subsequent to the prior bombing attack and under the protection of VIII *Flieger Korps*. This prerequisite was not met.

"It was not possible to have the group of Ju [52] aircraft, that returned between 09:00 and 10:00 from the first mission, ready for take-off by the ordered starting time of 13:00, and to have them leave punctually as one cohesive unit. The difficulties encountered with refueling, the removal of Ju aircraft that had broken down on the runway, the tremendous accumulation of dust on the fields and substantial losses of both personnel and machinery during the first mission, delayed the take-off of individual Ju groups by up to

This view of the Greek coastline is an indication of the low altitude at which the aircraft flew. Courtesy Moog Collection.

three and a half hours. Because the telephone connections between the fields had been interrupted, it was not possible to inform the commanding officers promptly about the delay that had occurred and determine a new collective take-off time. As a result of these factors, the units began their operations in the wrong tactical order and arrived over their objective areas not in unison, but in a staggered manner in relay units between 15:00 and 18:00. As the Me 110s were only able to arrive over their objective areas by 16:15 for reasons relating to range, the majority of the forces had to jump without Me 110 protection. The bombing attacks of the VIII.*Flg.Korps*

shortly before 15:00 had not destroyed the enemy, but rather kept the Allied troops temporarily under cover. Owing to the breakdown of machines during the first mission, the overall operational strength of the reinforced *Fallsch. Jg.Rgt.1* was unexpectedly reduced by around 600 men.

"The enemy (three English and two Greek battalions with a tank battalion) was also well-prepared to counter a parachute attack at Heraklion. Through skillful use of the terrain – which was deeply indented, rocky and cavernous – the opposing battalions surrounded the area around the airfield and the city of Heraklion by means of a comprehensively organized system of positions. They controlled the re-entrants [hollows], which alone were problematic for the drops, but on top of which the paratroopers had to contend with both head-on and flanking fire." *(Einsatz Kreta (Untenehmen Merkur) (Vorläufiger Erfahrungsbericht Gen. Kdo. XI. Fl. K. Abt. IA Br. B. Nr. 2981141 g.k. V. 11.06.1941) German Military Archives reference number RL 33/116.*

It is difficult to imagine a more seriously threatened start to an operation.

Finally, hours behind schedule, *Gruppe Ost* was ordered to board the waiting Ju 52s. By that stage of the day there were not enough aircraft to transport the two battalions and their supporting units in one lift. Not enough daylight remained for a second drop the same day, so some companies were left behind, again weakening an already understrength regiment. Regardless, the men clambered

A Ju 52 pilot checks his flight plan on the way to Crete. Courtesy Moog Collection.

aboard the aircraft, whose bare metal fuselages had, after standing in the sun, heated the cabins to a stifling level. Still, they were on the way. Gerhard Broder saw the Acropolis out of his window and alerted his comrades, but not one showed the slightest interest. They were all lost in their thoughts and Broder's went to two lines of the *Fallschirmjäger* song: *"The sun is shining red. Be ready!! You never know if she will be shining on us tomorrow."* (Broder interview, *op.cit.*). A close look at any of the many photographs taken on board the planes on the way to Crete shows that while there might have been some relief at being in the air finally, the tension and strain is immediately apparent on the men's faces. There are smiles, but they don't disguise the apprehension in the men's eyes. However, regardless of the uncertainties which lay ahead and the worry on some faces, the photographs also

Keeping good formation despite enemy fire, the Ju 52s drop their troops over the Heraklion area. Courtesy Moog Collection.

show groups of men with an unshakeable determination to carry out the mission.

Waiting for them were four British and Australian infantry battalions, six tanks from the 3rd Hussars and five from the 7th Royal Tank Regiment, three anti-aircraft batteries (light and heavy), two artillery batteries and two understrength Greek regiments. In addition, there were Engineers, Service and Ordnance Corps detachments and headquarters troops. In all, the Heraklion sector was defended by 8,000 Allied troops. They had been told to expect the Germans in the mid-afternoon and since then, with no sign of the enemy, there had been a feeling of anti-climax among the troops. That quickly changed at 17:30.

The 2nd Battalion The Black Watch was strongly entrenched in a horseshoe-shaped perimeter around the southeastern end of the airport. They had received reports at 14:30 that landings had begun at Maleme. At 16:00 bombers and Stukas appeared overhead their positions, but the deep and well-camouflaged positions gave excellent protection. The Stuka attack lasted only twenty minutes because of this aircraft's limited range, giving the defenders ample time to recover from the attack and prepare for the arrival of the paratroopers.

Fallschirmjäger approaching the ground near Heraklion. The position of the man in the foreground illustrates how different the German parachuting technique was from that of the Americans and British. The German paratrooper, arms by his side, has no directional control over his parachute. Courtesy Moog Collection.

Finally, at 17:29, Ju 52s were sighted approaching the airport. On board the planes the order to prepare to jump was given as the aircraft passed over the large rocky island of Dia, just off Heraklion's harbor. The men clambered to their feet, attached their static lines to the metal tube running along the ceiling of the cabin and braced themselves as the pilots banked for the run into the drop zone. The Scots and the Commonwealth troops in nearby positions watched in amazement as the sky suddenly filled with parachutes of different colors. At once the intense fire from the ground brought results as planes were seen slowly descending trailing fire, with paratroopers desperately trying to escape. Other aircraft quickly became deathtraps when flames engulfed the men as they tried to jump; many fell to their deaths as the silk parachutes disappeared in puffs of flame and smoke. Some aircraft simply exploded and the occupants were flung from the disintegrating wreckage. For those who had made successful exits from their aircraft there was now the horror of being shot at while descending. There was no possibility of shooting back or of maneuvering away; if you were lucky you made it to the ground alive. Those on the ground were at first

Paratroopers commandeer an Allied truck. Courtesy Moog Collection.

awestruck by the number of aircraft and the parachutes which seemed to fill the sky, but quickly they brought their weapons to bear on the frantically twisting and turning paratroopers; the fast-descending *Fallschirmjäger* were more difficult to hit than many soldiers had anticipated, but the sheer volume of fire inevitably found many targets.

Shrapnel and bullets started zipping through the aircraft, often finding human flesh in their trajectory. Even for the veterans, this must have been an utterly terrifying few minutes as they waited for the klaxon to sound the order to jump. In those moments there would have been an almost frantic desire to escape the aircraft, with the senses bombarded by the noise of aircraft engines, men's shouts, the air rushing past the open doorway; the sight of comrades torn by bullets and shrapnel; then at last the horn and the fast shuffle towards the exit. In an instant they felt the shock of the wind, followed seconds later by the spread-eagle dive, the harsh but reassuring jerk as the canopy opened, the sound of rounds breaking the sound barrier as they cracked past, the desperate twisting and turning to try to avoid the bullets, the ground rushing up, the crash onto the knees and the gathering in of the 'chute. The jump was over in seconds, but once on the ground another deficiency in the German parachute design brought additional danger: there was no quick release buckle for the harness, so time slowed as the men freed themselves from the 'chutes. At last, flat to the ground, they searched for comrades and weapons containers. And from everywhere came the cries of the wounded and the deafening sounds and acrid smells of the battlefield.

The official after action report described the perils of the jump:

Lebrecht in his Luftwaffe uniform in April 1941, aged nineteen, a month before his death. Courtesy Gertrud v. Ketelhodt.

"Several aircraft plummeted to the ground on fire. Owing to the drop height of 200 meters, which was necessary because of the terrain, many *Fallschirmjäger* were either wounded or killed in the air before they even reached the ground." (*Einsatz Kreta, op.cit.*).

For those who survived the descent, now came the real fight to survive. Again, it was all a matter of luck. For those who landed near weapons containers (parachutes of different colors helped the men identify what each container carried, but a risky dash across open and steel-swept ground was still necessary) and with a group of comrades, with cover nearby, away from enemy fields of fire, there was time to assess, regroup and prepare for action. If they were lucky they landed close to containers with weapons and grenades, or even light artillery pieces which descended under three parachutes. But for too many, landing brought them directly into the sights of the waiting British and Australian troops. While many Allied troops gleefully used hunting terms in their descriptions of trapping and killing groups of paratroops, and expressed their elation at the number of kills they had made, many others quickly became sickened at the slaughter. One Australian described the scene as, "… just like a duck shoot when they were coming down. One company had no less than 100 men killed in their sector; it was plain murder." (S.V. Dean, *Nasse*, p.120).

To the west of airport, *Gefreiter* Lebrecht von Blücher jumped with his 7th company of IIFJR1, commanded by *Oberleutnant* Herbert Karl Abratis. Like nearly all of his men, this was Abratis's first taste of combat. They landed among Australian infantry and several light and medium tanks. Australians on one of the Two Charlies described what happened:

> "Nine troop carriers came straight at us. There was a familiar series of explosions from the 'drome and we watched red streaks of tracer shells carrying upwards. The first plane was hit squarely on the nose and, bursting into flames, crashed on the shore. The next plane also caught fire and crashed in front of us before any paratroops had succeeded in jumping. The third was hit and caught fire, but blew up. The fourth plane burst into flames, the men jumped and most of their 'chutes opened but the flames from the burning plane seemed to reach down and I saw puffs of smoke as each parachute burned and the poor devils hurtled to their deaths. The fifth plane had its tail shot off and crash-landed just to our left; the troops jumped at about fifty feet and all were killed. The sixth plane dropped its men but was hit and almost crashed on us, passing over our heads with a bare six feet to spare and crashed fifty yards away. The rest of the planes were brought down on our right, so not one escaped." (Quoted in, Ben Christensen, *The History of The 1st Fallschirmjäger Division*, Volume 1, pp.182-3).

Another Australian soldier described, "… horrible scenes. Men jumping from machines and their parachutes not opening, others hang by the fuselage of the transport planes that were shot down at short range." (Christensen, p.183, *op.cit.*)

Within twenty minutes Lebrecht's company was wiped out, every man shot down as they tried to release their parachutes, run down by the advancing tanks, or if they were fortunate, dead before they hit the ground. Over 300 men were killed from the 6th and 7th companies; three wounded men were the only survivors of 6th company. Exactly how Lebrecht died would never be discovered. In a further sad twist, although he was identified and buried immediately after the fighting (see Aftermath), his remains were unaccountably lost and he is now listed on the Wall of the Missing at Maleme. The young man who loved sport, played musical instruments and devoured fine literature just disappeared. Nobody from his unit survived to report on how he died; there was no condolence letter from his company commander, as he too perished; there was to be no grave to give some substance to Lebrecht's memory. Of the three deaths, this was possibly the saddest of all, as the circumstances of his death would be forever a mystery. The German after action report described the fate of these men:

"The combat group situated west of the *II./Fallsch.Jg.Rgt.1*, which was under the command of *Hauptmann* Dunz, which consisted of the 6th and 7th [Lebrecht's] companies and *1./Fla.M.G.Batl.7*, and which parachuted onto the western edge of the airfield, was annihilated within 20 minutes. If the *Fallschirmjäger* were not killed or wounded in the air from heavy anti-aircraft, machine-gun and rifle fire, they succumbed to immediate attack from several light and intermediate tanks that drove in among the landing *Fallschirmjäger*. Only three men from the 6th Company and 2 men from the *Fallsch.Fla.-M.G.-Komp.* succeeded in battling their way to the regiment by swimming along the coast, and thus bringing information about the progression of the battle. In the battalion as a whole, 12 officers and 300 men had perished and 8 officers and 100 men had been wounded."

To the east of the airfield, the delays in leaving Topolia were to work in Wolfgang and Hans Joachim's favor. Only the 3rd company of the 1st battalion landed on time in the area around Gournes (east of the airport), whose radio station was the first objective. The 1st (Hans Joachim) and 2nd (Wolfgang) companies, together with *Major* Erich Walther's battalion headquarters group dropped three hours later, by which time the dropping zones had been moved further south-east and out of range of enemy fire. Gerhard Broder, a comrade of Wolfgang's, was on the same aircraft as Wolfgang and snapped a photograph of him minutes before the drop began. The surviving print is in poor condition, but considering that the camera that took the photo was damaged by a machine gun bullet from a British tank, it is fortunate that the photo exists at all. This was the only usable photo from the roll of film in the camera. In the photograph, Wolfgang also has a camera around his neck, as did many of the paratroopers. The poor quality of the print does not hide the apprehension on his face. It was the last photo taken of him. When the signal was given, Wolfgang was the first out of the Junkers; Gerhard Broder followed him at number four and recalled:

" We flew in at low altitude and then climbed to 80-100 meters for the jump. Now everything happens very quickly: 'Get ready!' We attach ourselves, steal a quick look towards the comrade behind us and we are ready to go. *Graf* Blücher is already standing at the door, looking tense, with a machine-pistol strapped to his chest. We jump in quick order.

"My parachute opens at about 30 meters. I hear the noise of machine guns and the salvos from snipers. No artillery is firing. Below are vineyards, olive trees and the coastal road. Only a few swings on the parachute, then I am landing gently in a ditch alongside

The last photograph taken of Wolfgang, minutes before the drop on Crete. His Oberleutnant's rank insignia is visible on his left sleeve and he has a camera slung around his neck. He is holding a lifejacket. Courtesy Paul Bernhard.

the road. While lying there I separate myself from the 'chute and head for the weapons container which is about thirty meters away. The area is rocky and dangerous for parachutists. The planes make a wide turn and return to Greece without loss. They have achieved their mission.

"But now something strange is happening. We find ourselves alone. *Oberfeldwebel* Möller assembles our group. He is from Schleswig-Holstein and of unusually large stature. Of course, he is nicknamed 'Baby-Möller.' We assemble at our position in order to defend in an easterly direction. Our platoon leader has disappeared with the rest of the platoon. He is marching towards Heraklion airport because there has been no contact with the enemy. At dawn our group decides to follow.

"Twelve men, injured during the jump, stay behind with a medic. Later we discover that the injured men had been killed and their bodies mutilated during the night by Greek civilians. The corpses are hastily buried. Is this now acceptable in war?" (Gerhard Broder, *Guerre Mondiale contre Moi,* pp.86-88; and Broder interview, *op.cit.*)

Their first objective, the radio station at Gournes, was quickly secured and the battalion then moved to the northwest to support the assault on the airfield. The battalion was missing its 4th company, which could not drop due to darkness and Wolfgang's company had dropped some five kilometers east of its intended target, the result of a navigation error by the lead pilots. According to the operation order, they were supposed to land near the airport at the Karteros River. His company linked up with the battalion headquarters later in the evening. The regimental staff headquarters group, with *Oberst* Bräuer, landed at 18:40 near Gournes and in a manner characteristic of *Oberst* Bräuer's leadership style, he immediately set out for the airfield, along the coastal road, with the aim of linking up with *Hauptmann* Burkardt's 2nd battalion, which had landed closer to the airport. At about 23:40, *Major* Walther received orders to assemble his battalion and also advance in the direction of the airport. It took time to gather the companies together and one platoon of the 1st company, commanded by *Leutnant* Lindenburg could not be located. Against orders Lindenburg had moved into mountains east of Gournes, where he and his men were attacked by Greek troops and irregulars. The platoon was wiped out. Due to command and control difficulties, the remainder of the battalion advanced in platoons and companies, rather than as a battalion *en masse*.

To provide protection for Bräuer's regimental command group, *Major* Walther assigned his best platoon commander and his men: *Oberleutnant* Wolfgang von Blücher. In the confusion of the landings, the poor communications and optimistic assumptions about the figures seen on the airfield, it was believed that the airfield was already in German hands. So in darkness, with just one platoon as protection, and no reconnaissance, the regimental commander led his party off in the direction of the airport. The sequence of events which resulted from this fateful order was described in some detail by one of the survivors of Wolfgang's platoon, *Oberfeldwebel* Schneider, in a book published in Germany in 1944, *Sprung über Kreta*. The account that follows is based on that narrative, the German after-action report and Wolfgang's comrade Gerhard Broder's recollections.

During the advance to the airport, small parties of British troops were found in vineyards and cornfields. These groups were dispatched with grenades and machine pistols. At around midnight Wolfgang's platoon sighted troops ahead on a hill to the southeast of the airport. Assuming they were members of Burkhardt's battalion, the platoon continued advancing, not realizing that they had somehow moved through the perimeter of the 2nd Battalion The Black Watch. While *Oberst* Bräuer established his regimental headquarters on the high ground two kilometers east of the airport, Wolfgang led his platoon through heavy enemy fire to high ground very near the eastern edge of the airfield. All of this was accomplished in darkness and over very

Commonwealth troops surrender after the Allied capitulation.
Courtesy Moog Collection.

Major Erich Walther, as he was when he commanded the 1st Battalion of the 1st Fallschirmjäger Regiment. He was battalion commander to both Wolfgang and Hans Joachim. Courtesy Fallschirmjäger archive, military archives, Freiburg.

rough terrain. Wolfgang and his men went to ground under heavy fire and tried to find cover in the hard, stone-filled ground. There was scattered scrub that offered some concealment, but it was impossible to dig body-deep foxholes for protection and even in the pre-dawn darkness casualties began to mount. The darkness and excellent camouflage made identifying the British positions very difficult. Despite this, Wolfgang ordered an assault on the enemy positions, in near total darkness. This attack succeeded in forcing the enemy to abandon positions on the southeastern slope at the edge of the airport.

Gerhard Broder was within sight Wolfgang's position:

"At dawn we reach a hill and we can now see the airport. In front of us there is a plain, covered with vineyards, which can be well covered by the enemy. Some shooting begins and green flares appear. Somebody shouts: 'Tanks ahead!'

"We realize that the airport has not been captured. We are under fire from

Commander of the 1st Fallschirmjäger Regiment Oberst Bruno Bräuer confers with his officers during the battle for Heraklion airfield. Courtesy Fallschirmjäger archive, military archives, Freiburg.

excellently camouflaged emplacements, strengthened by sandbags, manned by Englishmen who are not at all demoralized…

"… [*Ober-*] *Leutnant* Blücher has already crossed the plain during darkness and has penetrated the English positions. We have no communication with him and his men. He is under heavy fire from the British. The rocky terrain is the only protection he has from the enemy and from friendly fire too."

By daybreak on 21 May the precariousness of Wolfgang's position was obvious to observers in other units. *Oberst* Bräuer now appreciated the strength of the British defenses and he knew that only quick reinforcement of Wolfgang's platoon would allow his men to defeat the enemy. Wolfgang and his platoon were surrounded by well-entrenched Scottish infantry, who were supported by mortars and artillery. The paratroopers were exposed on rocky ground atop a flat-topped hill on which it was almost impossible to find cover. The equipment they jumped with did not include entrenching tools so the men were forced to scrape shallow foxholes with their helmets, all the while under fire. They had no MG-34 machine-guns and as the day broke and became hotter both lack of water and shortage of ammunition would become critical problems facing Wolfgang. As he had no communications

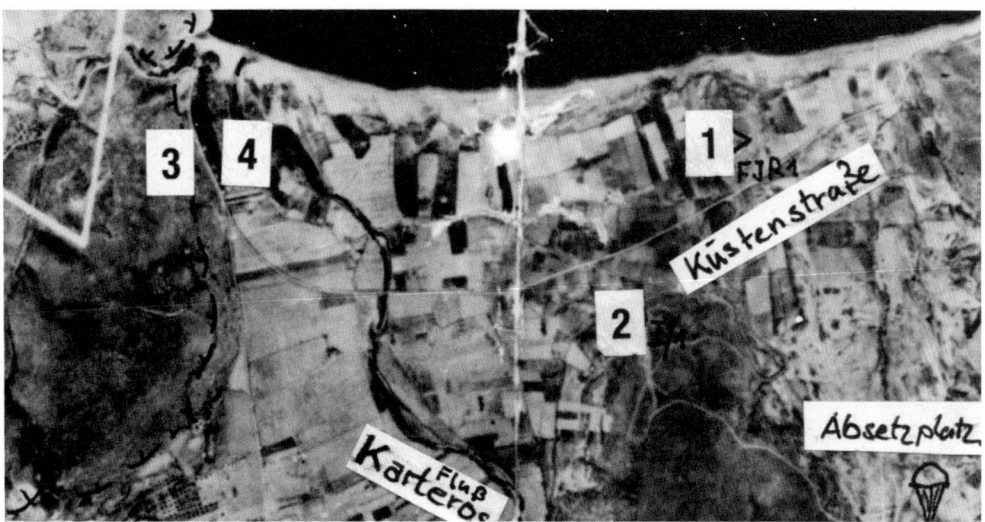

German photo reconnaissance map showing positions east of Heraklion airfield during the battle. Key to numbers: 1. Command post of 1st FJR Regiment; 2. Command post of 1st Battalion of 1st FJR Regiment; 3. Position of Wolfgang von Blücher's platoon, surrounded by the British; 4. Position where survivors of Wolfgang's platoon hid for nine days after the battle which took Wolfgang's life. The British defensive line is indicated in black ink near the numeral 3. Courtesy Paul Bernhard.

back to battalion headquarters, *Oberst* Bräuer returned to the battalion HQ and issued orders to *Major* Walther. But assembling a strong enough assault force from the scattered units took time and while Bräuer tried to put together enough men for a strong attack on the airfield, other men of Wolfgang's battalion tried desperately to rescue their comrades. This involved smaller units making individual attacks, all of which were unsuccessful. All the while, Wolfgang and his men were under accurate and heavy fire. Wolfgang was wounded in an arm, but a regimental doctor arrived with water and dressings for the injured men. By the early morning the assault that Bräuer had tried so desperately to organize had still not eventuated. With increasing light, any attack would lose the advantages of surprise and the cover of darkness. Wolfgang had no alternative but to order his men to prepare more substantial defensive positions in anticipation of enemy assaults. Meanwhile, the British had brought up two tanks, against which the two light anti-tank weapons carried by the platoon were ineffective.

It was while *Oberst* Bräuer was trying to reach Wolfgang's position that a revealing scene involving the veteran commander with a minor but distinctive stutter was described by a paratrooper alongside him:

> "'Daddy' Bräuer was standing there erect with a cigarette in a holder

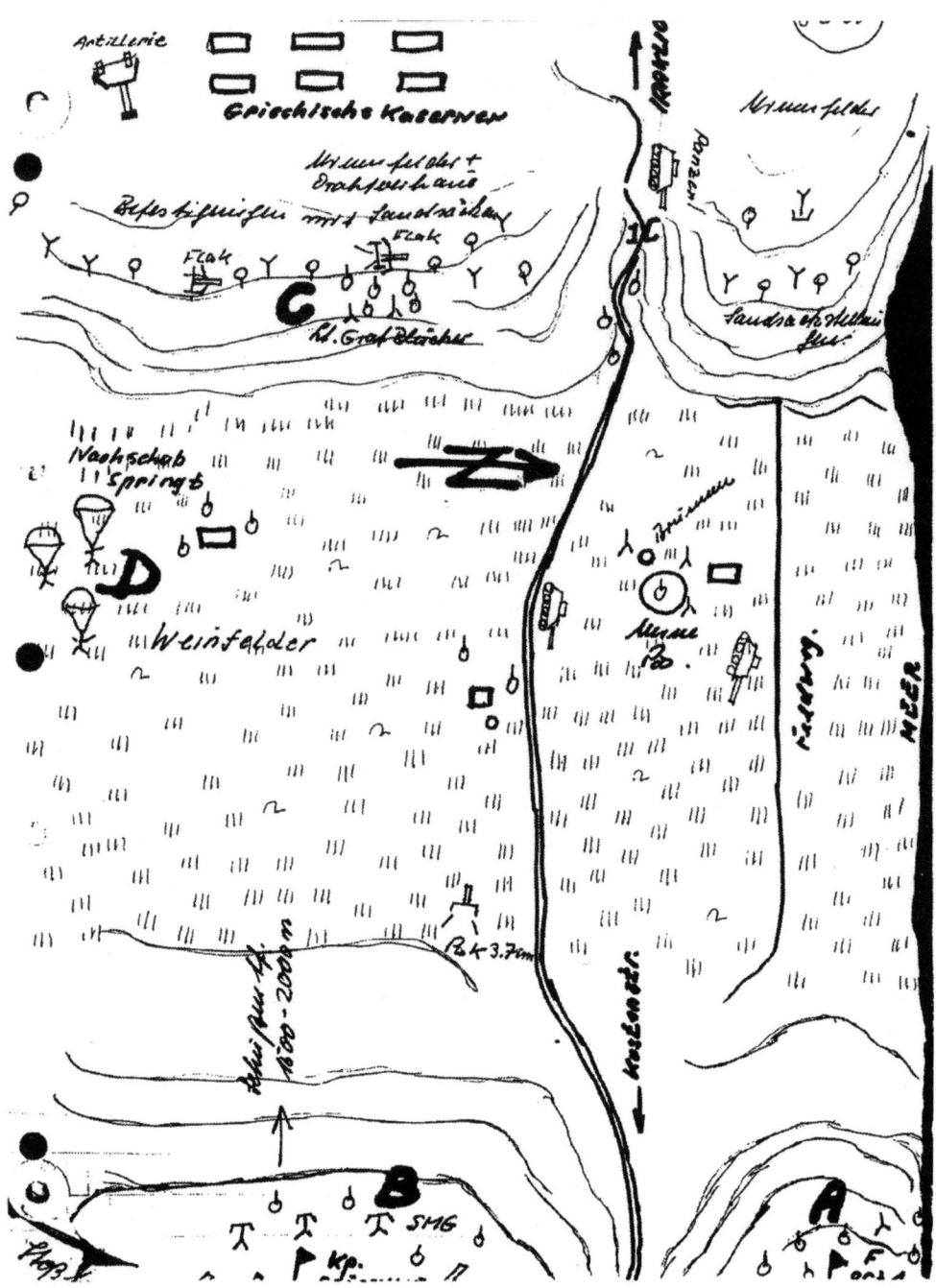

Gerhard Broder's hand-drawn map showing relevant positions near where Wolfgang and his platoon were besieged. Key to map: A. Battalion HQ; B. Heavy machine-gun position; C. Wolfgang's position; D. Supply drop area; "Meer" – the sea; "meine pos" – spot from where Gerhard Broder witnessed Wolfgang's death. Courtesy Paul Bernhard.

in his mouth in the midst of a hail of whistling bullets, and directed soldiers who had come singly to their positions. When I came up, I saw Alfred Schreiermann, second-in-command of our squad, lying at the feet of *Oberst Leutnant* Bräuer, digging himself in. At that moment I heard him yell with pain having been hit in the knee. I asked the colonel at least to take some cover behind the houses and this he did, and said with a dry humor: 'I think those fellows wanted to knock my cigarette out of my mouth.'" (Christensen, p.182, *op.cit.*)

Gerhard Broder was also close to the enemy:

"We are proceeding individually. I meet *Leutnant* Zeiler, who is now the battalion adjutant. He is gathering some men and suggests bypassing the English positions. We hurry southwards at an oblique angle to the enemy, thus presenting a difficult target. Our movement ends at a garden house, which is about half way to the airport. There we meet a group of lost paratroopers, some of whom are injured. The enemy positions cannot be captured under these conditions with the means available to us."

Unknown to Wolfgang, the battle for Crete had reached a critical turning point even as he and his men fought for their lives. Only seven thousand *Fallschirmjäger*, many of whom were dead or wounded, faced 43,000 Allied troops, but the tide was about to turn. At Maleme, the British delayed counterattacking the German paratroopers at the airfield and when they did attack with a small force it was easily repulsed. This result and misunderstandings among British commanders led to British forces withdrawing from their strong positions overlooking the airfield. While initial paratroop losses were so heavy that General Student considered withdrawing his forces, and much heavy fighting lay ahead over the next few days, the momentum of battle would now shift to the Germans. British troops were largely confined to their defensive positions to guard against expected attacks from the sea; the Allied reluctance to counter-attack gave the lightly armed paratroopers time to regroup and await the arrival of reinforcements. As soon as troops could be landed at Maleme airfield the aircraft began shuttling them in throughout the daylight hours to reinforce the paratroopers. With the new troops came light artillery pieces, mortars and machine guns. And with the mountain troops came the legendary *Oberst* Hermann Ramcke and his *Kampfgruppe* (battle group) of 550 men. After landing close to Maleme airfield they linked up with the paratroopers and the combined force took the airfield by early evening of 21 May. Now the massive reinforcement operation could continue uninterrupted by enemy fire, with continuous flights bringing in men, weapons and supplies.

Near Heraklion airport the situation was nowhere near as optimistic. While slow progress was made in Heraklion town, attempts to reach Wolfgang's platoon by Major Walther's 1st Battalion and by *Hauptmann* Burkhardt's men of the 2nd battalion were repulsed by the strong Black Watch defense. Because of delays caused by the time taken to locate and brief individual companies and platoons, *Oberst*

The entrance to a cave provided good protection from enemy fire. Courtesy Moog Collection.

Observing enemy positions from a safe defensive location. Courtesy Moog Collection.

A casualty station treating wounded men from both sides. Courtesy Moog Collection.

Advancing under fire using a stonewall for cover. Note the rocky terrain which made digging for cover under fire extremely difficult and hazardous. Courtesy Fallschirmjäger archive, military archives, Freiburg.

A light anti-tank gun in action. Courtesy Moog Collection.

Paratroopers resting after action. Courtesy Moog Collection.

Bräuer, who could see how desperate Wolfgang's position was, committed his force to battle piecemeal. Assaults by individual platoons and companies were easily beaten back by the British and one assault was devastated by heavy artillery and mortar fire while the men were assembling, causing heavy casualties.

The situation was untenable for Wolfgang and his men. A British anti-aircraft gun was firing over open sights at the German positions, wounding men and damaging weapons. The British position was heavily protected and the German light machine guns could do nothing to prevent this devastating rain of shells. By mid-morning ammunition was low and the platoon was at half strength. Wolfgang sent a runner to request urgent supplies of water and ammunition; he returned safely

Taking a break in a vineyard, but judging from the tense expressions on the faces of several of the men, the action is not far away. Courtesy Moog Collection.

through heavy fire and before collapsing from exhaustion, reported that help was on its way. Some men had resorted to drinking from a ditch, which quickly resulted in dysentery. In addition to the anti-aircraft gun, Wolfgang's men suffered a heavy bombardment from nine artillery pieces that the British had positioned to the west of the airfield. From all around the German platoon small arms fire poured from the well-camouflaged British positions keeping the relieving forces at bay, while continuing to kill and wound Wolfgang's men.

During one unsuccessful attempt to try to get to Wolfgang's position, Gerhard Broder noticed one of the *Gefreiters* carrying an MG-34, assisted by another man who was carrying ammunition canisters and pointing out targets. He wore the Knight's Cross underneath his jump smock and Broder immediately recognized his battalion commander, *Major* Erich Walther as the *Gefreiter's* assistant. That was illustrative of Walther's style of leadership, but it was also an indication of how desperate he was to save Wolfgang and his platoon. (Broder, p.90, *op.cit.*).

Late in the morning occurred the battle's most celebrated and extraordinary event, one that was to result in an enduring myth among Cretans living in the area.

In the first company of the 1st Battalion was Wolfgang's youngest brother, Hans Joachim. As a member of the force trying to reach Wolfgang, Hans Joachim was only 300 meters from Wolfgang's position. He watched helplessly as repeated assaults failed to get through to the besieged platoon. It

A command post with a radio operator at center. His radio is still in its impact-absorbing container. Note the bandolier (ammunition pouches) draped around the neck of the man at right; this was one of many pieces of equipment which was unique to the Fallschirmjäger. Courtesy Moog Collection.

was obvious that the complete destruction of the platoon was imminent.

As Wolfgang and his men prepared to make their last stand the heavy British fire faltered suddenly. From the German lines came an amazing sight: a farm horse galloping along a road, ridden bareback by a young paratrooper with total disregard for his own life. Draped over the horse's neck and over its back were canisters of ammunition. As the horse and its rider neared the German position the British troops began firing again; rounds were hitting the ground ahead of and behind the horse and within seconds, inevitably, both horse and rider were cut down. One of Wolfgang's men immediately ran down the slope to the wounded man and dragged him off the road and into bushes.

This courageous man then returned to the platoon's position, miraculously unharmed and carrying the ammunition containers that had been hung over the horse. The rider had died but the vital ammunition reached the besieged platoon. Now the soldier who had scrambled down to the fallen horse and rider hesitantly reported to Wolfgang von Blücher that the gallant horse rider had been his seventeen-year-old brother, Hans Joachim. The soldier paused, then added that Hans Joachim had been hit by a machine gun bullet and had not suffered. Wolfgang's face tightened, he grasped the hand of the distraught soldier, then turned his attention to observing enemy positions through his field glasses.

Many Internet sites incorrectly name the rider as Lebrecht, who had been killed

Part Four - Crete

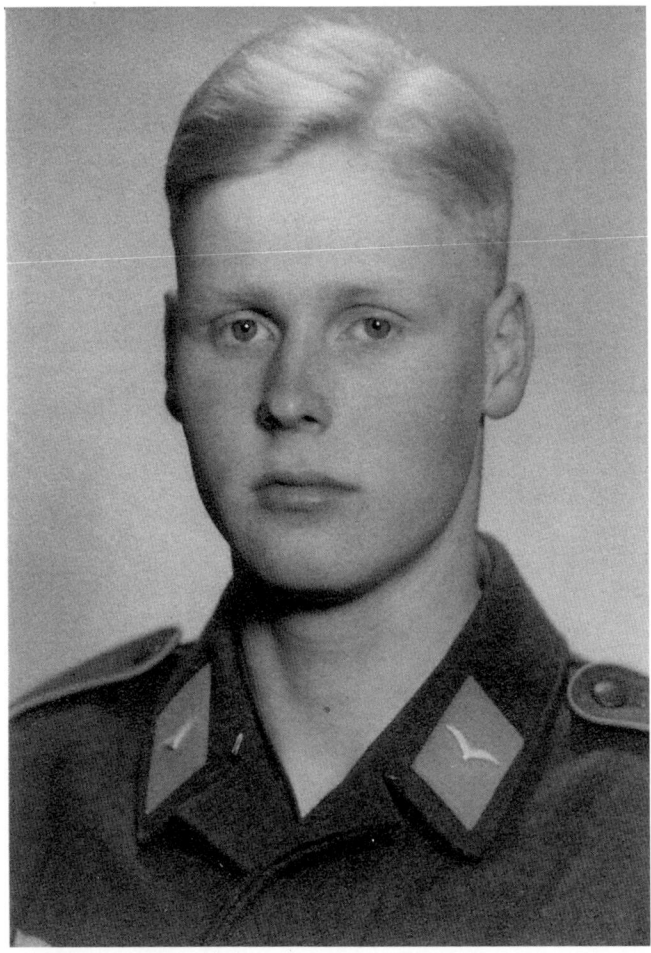

Hans Joachim, aged seventeen, in his Luftwaffe uniform in April 1941, two months before his death. Courtesy Gertrud v. Ketelhodt.

with the rest of his company on the western side of the airport the previous day. It was reported that for years afterwards, locals saw a soldier riding a horse in a ghost-like scenario. The Cretans at first believed the rider was a British officer, but over time this changed to a German paratrooper.

This dramatic and heroic event epitomized Hans Joachim's courage, athleticism and even his foolhardiness, but remarkably the von Blücher family was never informed of the exact details of Hans Joachim's death. Gertrud (their sister) remembers that the family was told that Hans Joachim was killed while trying to help his brother Wolfgang, but no more than that. Gerhard Broder, who watched Wolfgang in his last minutes through his field glasses did not witness the event. And, in Helmuth Steger's memoir of Hans Joachim (see the Aftermath) he quotes an unnamed paratrooper who describes Hans Joachim's death in some detail, but makes no mention of a dramatic horse ride.

While there appears to be only one report by an eyewitness of Hans Joachim's courageous action, it would certainly have been in character for Hans Joachim to have taken such a dramatic and dangerous course of action in trying to assist the brother whom he idolized. Like many headstrong teenagers he was a young man of contradictory qualities. In the course of my interview with his sister, she described him as modest and very fair-minded, but also as audacious, athletic, brave and strong. His action did not change the outcome of the battle for Wolfgang, but it did provide an astonishing example of raw courage and this in turn resulted in the local people maintaining the memory of his legendary ride for years afterwards.

At noon, the British began a final assault on Wolfgang's position. With the anti-aircraft gun pounding the Germans in their shallow scrapes, the enemy infantry approached to within about fifty meters of the position. Wolfgang's men reported to him that they had run out of ammunition. They expected that he would now surrender. Instead he reminded his men that they had been ordered to hold their position and that his orders were to hold even until death. The platoon's strength was now eighteen men, eleven of whom were wounded. The British realized this and poured rounds into the German positions. Without grenades or ammunition the men could only cower in their meager shelters. Wolfgang cast his eyes over his men, then crept out of his hole towards a dead British soldier. As he returned with the man's weapon and ammunition he was hit and fell to his side. He did not speak, but his hands continued to grip the British weapon. Watched by their comrades who were unable to relieve the platoon, the remnants of Wolfgang's platoon were about to be overwhelmed by infantry and supporting tanks. *Oberfeldwebel* Schneider attached a handkerchief to his light machine gun and held it up. From three hundred meters away Gerhard Broder and his comrades were watching Wolfgang's men through their field glasses:

> "We could see that *Leutnant* von Blücher's men were surrendering. The soldiers were going into captivity and the English were taking over the position … *Graf* von Blücher did not put his hands up. He raised himself up from his cover, showing his striking blond hair. He was immediately shot in the head … *Feldwebel* 'Baby-Möller' had tried to join Blücher and he too was killed in action."

In Gerhard Broder's view, the manner of Wolfgang's death was inexcusable: "He [the British] was not threatened, his enemy was unarmed and in a hopeless situation, at the end of his strength! This act was unsoldierly, not justified by any convention." (letter from G. Broder to Lebrecht von Blücher, June 2012).

This account of Wolfgang's death, which differs from *Oberfeldwebel* Schneider's, accords with what his sister Gertrud was told when she visited Stendal later in 1941 to meet with *Major* Walther. Near Wolfgang's body was that of his loyal sergeant, Möller, who had served with him since the invasion of Holland and who had made a final, desperate dash to help his commander. It would be nine days before German paratroops would be able to regain his position and retrieve the bodies. Incredibly,

Paratroopers passing a knocked-out British light tank. Courtesy Moog Collection.

three of Wolfgang's men who survived the final attack took refuge just a few meters from British positions where they were able to stay alive until found by their comrades. It is perhaps worth noting that while there were instances of "unsoldierly" conduct on Crete, there were also many recorded incidents that illustrated the humanity of men on both sides. Wounded soldiers were treated in British and German medical facilities without regard for nationality; some paratroopers were saved from a brutal death at the hands of civilians by the intervention of Allied officers; and it is evident that both sides had great respect for the fighting abilities of their opponents.

Once the battle for the airport was won, Gerhard Broder walked over the broken ground where Wolfgang's platoon had made their stand. It was already called "Blücherberg" (Blücher's hill). He described the scene of the battle: "Only now can we appreciate the unbelievable sadness of the scene. The whole airport area is engulfed by the intense, sweet smell of dead bodies … The place had been prepared with minefields, barbed-wire entanglements, tanks dug-in and anti-aircraft artillery. Whereas the British positions were strengthened with sand bags and were very well camouflaged, the German positions had no cover." (Broder, p.97, *op.cit.*).

The survivors buried their dead comrades with great reverence and respect. Elaborate crosses were erected, upon which rested the men's helmets. Word quickly got around that Lebrecht too had been killed, causing great sorrow in the regiment.

That day, 21 May, had brought tragedy for the von Blücher family, but the wider battle around Heraklion was

Confident paratroopers on the road, carrying ammunition pouches and armed with the venerable and widely-issued Karabiner 98k rifles. Courtesy Moog Collection.

Using local transport to help carry equipment. Courtesy Moog Collection.

Thick brush slowed progress in places. The man in front has discarded his woolen pants in favor of shorts, probably captured from Allied stores. Both men are armed with MP-40 sub-machine guns. The man at rear is wearing a pistol on his belt, carried by all paratroopers, and pouches for his MP-40 magazines can also be seen on his back. Courtesy Moog Collection.

Officers gathered at a makeshift command post. Both first and second pattern (with front lacing) jump boots can be seen on these men. Courtesy Moog Collection.

slowly turning to the Germans. They had strongly engaged all the Allied positions and as reinforcements, with heavy weapons, arrived safely out of the range of enemy fire, it became clear to the Allied commanders that despite their early successes, their position was fast becoming untenable. In addition, the German troops were assisted by a disagreement between British commanders, resulting in the Black Watch battalion delaying an attack on the German positions east of the airfield. This provided valuable breathing space for Bräuer's men and also enabled reinforcements to arrive via a temporary landing strip constructed out of range of Allied guns. That reinforcements and supplies arrived at all speaks to the courage of the Ju 52 pilots and their crews, who landed and took off under heavy fire at Maleme airfield, operated into roughly constructed temporary strips built hastily by paratroops and put their aircraft down

An exhausted Leutnant rests after a battle. Courtesy Moog Collection.

on beaches in order to bring desperately needed supplies to isolated units.

By late afternoon transports were landing non-stop at Maleme, bringing heavier weapons and fresh troops. Though much hard fighting remained before the standoff at Heraklion was resolved, the Allies began the evacuation of their troops on 25 May (though Heraklion town and airport would not be fully in German hands until 29 May), when General Freyberg realized that a German victory was inevitable. Around Heraklion unit cohesion among Allied troops was breaking down as a result of confused and contradictory orders. As discipline suffered, units began to withdraw without orders from their positions in an effort to reach evacuation points. According to the Allied commander, General Freyberg, "There were units sticking together and marching with weapons – units of one or other of the composite forces which had come out of the line – but in the main it was a disorganized rabble making its way doggedly and painfully to the South." (Christensen, p.228, *op.cit.*) Nevertheless, despite poor radio communications and some breakdown in discipline among non-combat troops, some 17,000 men had been evacuated by the time of the official surrender on 1 June. Smaller groups were still being evacuated several months later.

In less than two weeks the German invasion force had defeated an Allied defense with six times as many men. Numbers of Germans killed were twice those of the Allies, at 6,368, but the final tally added over 11,000 prisoners to the Allied casualty

A Ju 52 which crash-landed during the Crete operation. Courtesy Moog Collection.

Paratroopers observing enemy positions. Courtesy Moog Collection.

list. The mission had been accomplished, but at terrible cost. Hitler had been correct in his prediction and never again would the *Fallschirmjäger* carry out such large-scale airborne assaults. For the most part they would be consigned to infantry duty, where they fought with great distinction in places as distant as Russia, Italy, northern France and Tunisia.

The Battle of Crete has been the subject of controversy (mainly concerning decisions made by Allied commanders) for many years. Both sides in the Crete operation committed grave errors of planning and judgment and the tactics and decisions made by both the Germans and the Allies are still studied and analyzed at staff colleges. Pushing controversies to

The battle won: the smiling face of an Oberfeldwebel. Courtesy Moog Collection.

one side, the battle's outcome is without question a tribute to the qualities that the German *Fallschirmjäger* and their ground troop comrades brought to an operation in which they were inferior in numbers and in weaponry. Many of the Allied troops were not combat ready and others were service units, ill-equipped to face German paratroops. But there were some very effective Commonwealth units, such as the New Zealanders, which fought with great vigor. That the German force prevailed despite hopelessly inaccurate intelligence estimates, flawed planning and execution, despite the lack of heavy weapons, despite the fact that they were ill-equipped for the climatic conditions and despite the heavy casualties, suggests that in the end,

Comrades pay their respects to Wolfgang and his sergeant.
(Courtesy the Shaun Winkler Collection)

it was the leadership displayed by NCOs and officers and the fighting quality of the men on the ground which carried the battle. This achievement is all the more impressive when one remembers that they defeated an opponent who knew virtually every detail of the German invasion plan before the operation began and enjoyed the advantages of well-constructed defensive positions. It was a stunning victory.

Martin Pöppel summed up the Crete experience for the *Fallschirmjäger* bluntly:

> "The enemy had many more men on Crete than we did. Their numerical superiority had only been defeated by the unbroken spirit, the unbreakable will of all our men. But this episode was *not* [Pöppel's italics] a glorious chapter in the history of our supreme leadership; instead it was a glorious chapter in the history of each and every fighting man, whether he was a paratrooper, mountain infantryman, flyer or sailor. And each man honestly deserved his Iron Cross First Class [this decoration was awarded to every man who fought on Crete]." (Martin Pöppel, p.67, *op.cit.*)

General Student, writing after the war, said of the Crete operation:

> "It is difficult for me to write about the Battle for Crete. For me, as the commander of the German air-landed

Some of the many graves of dead Fallschirmjäger. After each battle, the dead were buried close to where they fell. Courtesy Moog Collection.

forces that conquered Crete, this name is a bitter memory. I miscalculated when I recommended this attack, and this not only meant the loss of many paratroopers, who were my sons, but also, in the end, the death of the German airborne force, which I had personally created." (quoted in Kurowski, p.165)

General Student's post-war understanding of Wolfgang's intention was that he had tried to take the airport by surprise on the evening of 20 May and despite strong resistance he and his men actually reached the southeast border of the airport. Finding themselves surrounded by a force with far superior firepower, the paratroopers dug in as best they could, hoping that their

Sounding the alarm call. This paratrooper carries a map case on his belt. Bundesarchiv.

Victorious paratroopers after the capture of Heraklion. Courtesy Moog Collection.

comrades would be able to break through the British line and relieve them. (Broder, p.280, *op.cit.*)

In the opinion of officers around him, Student aged noticeably during the touch-and-go of the first week of the operation. When he arrived on Crete he received a briefing from senior officers, but characteristically he quickly made for the NCOs and enlisted men to get their opinions on what had occurred. What he heard evidently shocked him, as then *Hauptmann Freiherr* (Baron) Friedrich von der Heydte (who wrote a fine memoir of his experiences on Crete, *Daedaelus Returned: Crete 1941*) recounted:

"… the general knew as well as anyone that this was an experiment with blood and human life. If he had not been convinced of the necessity of the experiment he would never have dared to attempt it. His primary aim was to spare the lives of his men. He was like no other general with his soldiers. He knew most of them personally, knew their good and bad sides, their wishes, and their troubles. He felt and suffered with them." (Christensen, p.223, *op.cit.*)

Wearing tropical kit, a platoon of Fallschirmjäger form up prior to a victory march. Courtesy Moog Collection.

For one family, the von Blüchers, the larger picture of a stunning German victory over vastly superior forces, was of little consequence. *Freifrau* (Baroness) Countess Gertrud von Nordheim (formerly Countess von Blücher) had received a letter from her son *Graf* Wolfgang in Athens, dated 19 May. Since then she had heard nothing. And the *Fallschirmjäger* were beginning to return home.

A paratrooper is decorated after the island had been secured. The pocket which held his "gravity" knife is clearly visible on the man's right pants leg. Courtesy Moog Collection.

Flying away from Crete, this shot captures the profile of a contemplative Fallschirmjäger. Courtesy Moog Collection.

Part Five
Aftermath

Order of the Day
Crete Warriors, Comrades!

A glorious deed in the history of our new branch has come to a conclusion. Victory flags wave on Crete. You, paratroopers and air-landed forces, together with comrades from the army, have accomplished once-in-a-lifetime deeds under your tried-and-true leaders of all ranks.

Airmen, paratroopers and mountain troops, in the spirit of brothers-in-arms, have forced the island of Crete in a manner reminiscent of those great days at Narvik and, as a result, have ejected England from important positions in the Mediterranean.

Comrades! All Germans are filled with the deepest admiration and unending thanks for your latest victory. Along with the Luftwaffe, all of the German Army is moved by and proud of the heroes who sacrificed their lives and their well being in the fighting for Crete.
Forward in the spirit of the victors of Crete!

Hermann Göring,
Reichsmarschall
(Quoted in Kurowski, p.164, *op.cit.*)

News of the costly victory on Crete appeared in German newspapers and other media days after the island was secured. The troops began returning home soon afterwards and welcome home/victory parades were held through the streets of the garrison towns that hosted *Fallschirmjäger* bases. The men wore tropical kit for the most part and their faces and limbs displayed the deep tan that advertised their Mediterranean exploit. They marched proudly, wearing the Iron Crosses awarded to all the survivors. But as they marched and received the ecstatic cheers of townsfolk, their thoughts must have been with their comrades who should have been marching with them, who were now in Cretan soil. These thoughts must have stayed with the survivors, even as they celebrated their victory and their survival. For now they could look forward to a period of leave at home, but soon enough they would be back at their bases for re-equipping, training and integrating the many replacement men required by the battered battalions. In fact there would be little respite from action for many of these veterans, but for a time they could relax with families and friends, recover their physical health and most importantly, they could attempt to find a place in their memories for all that they had seen, experienced and lost on Crete. They were welcomed home as heroes, but behind the smiles and the war stories were the all-too vivid reminders in their thoughts and

Part Five - Aftermath

The main gate at the Fallschirmjäger barracks, Gardelegen (near Stendal). A banner welcomes home the victors of Crete and a group of young boys wait to cheer the men. Courtesy Moog Collection.

Preparing for the victory march at Gardelegen, with the men wearing tropical uniforms. Courtesy Moog Collection.

dreams of what they had been through: the terror of the jump; seeing comrades' bodies torn apart by shrapnel, machine-gun rounds or mutilated by guerrillas; the prolonged deprivation of water and food; the desperate brutality of hand-to-hand combat; and for the many young men for whom Crete was their introduction to war, the loss of any kind of romanticism they may have held about battle. Such experiences could only be discussed with their comrades who had seen the same things. These were very tough men, but they were men; and they suffered.

For the families of casualties, including Gertrud von Nordheim, however, the wait for news of her sons was agonizingly long. Since the letter from Wolfgang, there had been nothing. As the days and weeks passed she and her daughters began to suspect the tidings could only be bad; perhaps one or more had been wounded? Or had been posted missing?

The news, when it came, was devastating. The day the letter containing the awful details arrived, Gertrud and her sister Elisabeth were in Berlin. Their mother was home with their stepfather, but the sisters hurried home when the news reached them. Their mother had believed that, no doubt like the vast majority of mothers of soldiers, all three of her sons would return safely. According to Gertrud, her mother never really came to terms with the fact that her sons would never return. For the rest of her life the fate of her sons weighed heavily on their mother, her health suffered and the grief never lifted, though she did find the strength to carry on through the war and the further tragedies it brought. Her life was to be torn apart once again when she learned that her husband had been taken prisoner by the Russians. In some ways, said Gertrud, her mother's life ended on the day she received news of the deaths of her sons. But, Gertrud believes, she and the rest of the family found the inner means to go on, just as other families did; in wartime you had to expect this sort of occurrence, even if you wanted to believe that it would never happen to your family; and like so many other mothers, the von Blüchers' eventually became stoical about her great loss, while never really coming to terms with it.

Finally, a month after the invasion had begun, *Oberst* Bräuer's letter to Elisabeth (the eldest daughter) arrived. It was followed several weeks later by *Major* Walther's handwritten letter to the brothers' mother, Gertrud von Nordheim.

The family followed German tradition and published an elaborately designed, but matter-of-fact death notice in the newspapers. At that stage of the war the deaths of three brothers in a single twenty-four hour period on the same field of battle would have been a most unusual occurrence; by the time the notice was published Operation Barbarossa (the invasion of the Soviet Union) had been launched and the days of comparatively light casualties for the German people would soon be forgotten. Even the heavy losses among the *Fallschirmjäger* on Crete would look insignificant after the momentous battles on the Eastern Front. There were some staggering victories to come in the war against the Soviet Union, but the defeats and the unbelievable losses that accompanied them followed soon after. And the war would continue to take its toll on the von Blücher family. Now, however, in June 1941, the family had to come to terms with this most unimaginable outcome.

First Parachute Regiment, Iraklion, 4th June 1941
Commander

My Very Dear Countess!
I deeply regret having to be the messenger of such devastating news, that during the attack on Crete, all three brothers, Wolfgang, Lebrecht and Hans Joachim were killed in action.

I personally advanced to the front on the evening of 20 May with Wolfgang. He had already received a slight, grazing

> Es starben den Heldentod auf Kreta unsere geliebten Söhne, Brüder, Enkel und Neffen
>
> der Ritterkreuzträger
>
> **Wolfgang Graf von Blücher**
> Oberleutnant in einem Fallschirmjägerregiment im Alter von 24 Jahren
>
> **Leberecht Graf von Blücher**
> Gefreiter in einem Fallschirmjägerregiment im Alter von 19 Jahren
>
> **Hans=Joachim Graf von Blücher**
> Jäger in einem Fallschirmjägerregiment im Alter von 17 Jahren.
>
> Darze, Post Stuer, in Mecklenburg
> Posen und Altengottern, den 23. Juni 1941
>
> Gertrud v. Nordheim, geb. Freiin Marschall, verw. Gräfin Blücher
> Ludwig v. Nordheim, Gaulandwirt im Luftgau II
> Elisabeth Gräfin v. Blücher
> Adolf Graf v. Blücher, Leutnant zur See
> Gertrud Gräfin v. Blücher
> Richenza v. Nordheim
> Wilhelmine Freifrau Marschall, geb. Gräfin Rittberg
> Charlotte Freiin Marschall

The von Blücher family's press notice announcing the deaths of three of its sons. Courtesy Fallschirmjäger archive, military archives, Freiburg.

wound. Then he continued advancing during the night with a few men towards the Iraklion airport and held his ground the next day in sweltering heat. For the next nine days there was no further communication with him, until we finally took the airport. We then found him dead among his fallen comrades with a shot to his head. He must have been killed in action on the 21st or 22nd of May. Even there he was possessed by an unquenchable drive to succeed and he would have been in line for another Knight's Cross for his courage.

Hans Joachim was killed in action during the attack by the 1st company on 21 May at the edge of the airport, approximately 300 meters from Wolfgang. He also excelled through his outstanding courage.

Lebrecht jumped with the 7th company on the western side of the airport. He died a heroic death together with the entire company.

The Regiment is proud of these three heroes. Their deeds and glory are everlasting.

May it serve as consolation to you, my dearest Countess, that these fallen soldiers fulfilled their duty, which was inherent in their name.

May I ask you to convey to your mother, your brother and your sister the deeply felt

Wolfgang's first grave, where he was buried alongside his platoon sergeant. Courtesy Gertrud v. Ketelhodt.

condolences of the entire Regiment. With deepest respect and constant concern, I am your extremely devoted, (signed) B. Bräuer

(Letter addressed to Countess Elisabeth v. Blücher, eldest sister of the brothers and received at Posen on 23 June 1941)

This letter was followed by one handwritten by *Major* Walther, a letter that he later told Gertrud, younger sister of the brothers, he could hardly bear to write. He said that he would, for the rest of his life, regret that he could not bring the brothers, especially the youngest, Hans Joachim, home to their family:

1st Battalion, 1st Parachute Regiment, Stendal (Altmark), 28/6/1941 Commander

My Dearest Lady,
 After my return from Crete, it is my deepest wish, my dearest lady, to express my most deep condolences and those of all the comrades of your outstanding sons,

Lebrecht's grave, soon after his death. The later whereabouts of his remains are a mystery. Courtesy Gertrud v. Ketelhodt.

Hans Joachim's first grave, on the left. Courtesy Gertrud v. Ketelhodt.

with regard to the great loss which the Battle of Crete has brought you.

Your sons were heroes in the battle and remained heroes in death. Even a mother has to show heroism when she must bear the news that fate has torn from her in one day, three children in the prime of their lives. You are surely not in a frame of mind to receive consolation. However, it is only fair and just that I am compelled to draw your attention to the fact that your sons were soldiers and warriors of a very special kind. They have fulfilled everything to the perfection that can be expected of a Blücher. Wolfgang and Hans Joachim were in my battalion. The youngster became in such a short time the favorite of us all; he longed ardently for battle and was blissfully happy when it finally began. What I would give if I had the chance to return such splendid boys to you.

Of course, we in the battalion had a very special relationship with Wolfgang. We shared in the superb operations in Norway [Dombas, April and Narvik, June 1940], Holland [May 1940] and through the many dangers we weathered, we had bonded in wonderful camaraderie. He was always the center of attention and his appearance always brought success; he was a rarely gifted officer and a successful soldier. And so his heroic death was also a tragic moment. Unfortunately, his loyal staff sergeant, Möller, who had stood steadfastly by his side in Holland at the time he gained his Knight's Cross, was also killed.

My very dearest Lady, the lives of your sons were short, but they gave their lives a deep meaning by living and fighting heroically and by giving in the end, to their people and to their fatherland the greatest that a human being is capable of giving. Their names will always be part of the history of our regiment. We will always show loyalty to our dead and always feel connected to the members of their families.

I beg you also to convey my deepest condolences to your young daughters. I remain in deep adoration your forever devoted,
Walther
Major and Commander of the Battalion

When the family travelled to Stendal to seek more information about the boys' deaths they met with *Oberst* Bruno Bräuer. Gertrud remembers that his account of Wolfgang's death was delivered very matter-of-factly, even coldly. She was surprised and offended by the manner in which the information was conveyed. She thought that perhaps *Oberst* Bräuer's letter had been written by an aide and was just one of many written by this person; hence the lack of any personal warmth. By contrast, Major Walther's letter was hand-written and demonstrates a close knowledge of Wolfgang and Hans Joachim. His sense of personal loss is obvious in both the tone and content of the letter. Later, in 1941, somebody in the 1st *Fallschirmjäger* Regiment sent Gertrud a set of photographs, including those of her sons' first graves and of the dedication ceremony for the original war cemetery.

News of the deaths reached Hans Joachim's school at Misdroy and must have been greeted with dismay and great sadness by all who knew him. His boarding housemaster, who would have known him better than anyone other staff member at the school, made an extraordinary effort to memorialize Jochen. He typed an eight page, single-spaced reminiscence about Jochen, sent to his mother, in which he relates incidents that occurred at the school and Jochen's part in them. It is a most unusual document and one that reveals several important facets of Jochen's character which would be seen vividly in his very short military career. The writer of the document, Helmuth Steger, obviously saw in Jochen a young man of rough edges but great promise; and it is clear that after some disciplinary problems had been resolved, Steger and Jochen became close friends. While Steger's emotions so soon after Jochen's death inevitably colored the memoir, his insights into Jochen's personality are fascinating and the portrait of Hans Joachim that emerges is both moving and full of thoughtful observations. It demands careful and reflective reading.

Jochen: An Intermezzo
A story by Helmuth Steger
In memoriam Hans-Joachim *Graf* von Blücher

When he suddenly arrived one day as the "New One", slim, blond, very fair, no, white-blond, of medium size and of an elastic bounciness all over his body, a bit cheeky in his conduct but not without modesty – that's when I knew that we would become friends; because the courageous manner of the boy took me captive. I could feel his recklessness. I soon realized: he has adventure in his blood; he needs danger, because then he is in his element. Whenever others begin to feel a bit queasy, around the stomach area, when their knees want to give in, then and particularly then will courage gleam laughingly in his blue eyes. That's what I thought and that's what came to pass. But he was still just a boy.

His body showed it sooner than his spirit, and soon he proved his disposition during his physical exercise. He came from the country and had never done apparatus gymnastics; he neither knew some of them by name nor by appearance, he knew of no formal exercise, but the natural lightness of all of his movements, the unhindered flexibility of this willowy, steely body, proved to the experienced eye to be the born gymnast, the fast runner, the talented athlete. Is it surprising then that he stood out in the foreground during these brief weeks, that one or the other companionable eye wandered in the direction of this elegant newcomer, who was lithe yet strong, strong but not heavy? It didn't take long and his exercises had the same effortless dispassion, this mechanically flowing manner that is only owned by the original talent and the bravely limited, the diligently striving, often to the point of exacerbation … That's how Jochen soon led a gymnastic team. He was soon known as somewhat of a gymnastics authority, he had settled so completely into our division that one could only with difficulty imagine him not being there, until one good, bad day more adventure tempted him.

Although only in grade six, although only the youngest of four brothers, of whom three are already serving the flag, although I drew his attention to it over and over again that he would be fetched, if needed, without fail not just him, but every other one of us as well, who was needed, despite all "althoughs" the war has now taken his peace of mind. More and more does his soldier-like, his toned nature egg him on, that wants to surge, wants action, physical, visible action and no contemplation or observation of things whatsoever. I clearly notice how far from my nature this kind of uncompromising manner is, at least how it seems to be in Jochen's blood, how he acts without knowing where it comes from, but with the brave unbroken power of a person, who gets a scent of his element. One can feel the grandson and great-grandson of Prussian officers and undoubtedly also the aristocrat. Thereafter, I call him by his surname.

He, who is seventeen and a half, is slender and wheat blond, who looks fresh and florid and has no room for fear in his

Hans Joachim, aged fourteen, in the summer of 1938. Courtesy Gertrud v. Ketelhodt.

eyes; yes, how could he not be extraordinarily well-liked by his comrades? Despite being often big-mouthed at first, Jochen more and more won everyone's heart: because he was first of all and last of all a comrade and to top it all the boldest and most courageous of them all. When he received a parcel and somebody came to visit him in his room, even someone he didn't like, he shared with him. If something was said, especially by a teacher, against someone who wasn't present, Jochen was the first to carry his torch. He felt for the one under attack, he immediately defended him from the core of his being, and that's why it seemed so empathic and blameless. During a fire in the night, the flames are reaching high up into the air: compared with other students, he extinguishes in a dangerous place. When he fastens the roof antenna, it seems like a miracle that he comes climbing down unscathed, that's how far he dared go up without a safety rope. After two weeks of apparatus gymnastics, he does without much ado, just by the way, the straddle down from the high bar. He dares to do everything that can be dared: he takes part in all the pranks; he welcomes every opportunity to break the rules. So, inevitably, we will have to confront each other sometime.

The quietest and least active times at a boarding school are the Sundays. One has nothing to do with bugle calls and probably also forgets about school. Therefore some call them the dead times. That's when one walks into the beautiful, big and near forest, one trudges, one dawdles. But sometimes, around the beginning of January, one also goes ice-skating, when the [Baltic] sea is frozen. That has been forbidden more than once and is therefore tempting and that a certain Jochen will be found among the ice-skaters, is self-evident. Because where else would he be, if something is forbidden?

So, five of them headed out on a cold Sunday in January straight after lunch, from the boarding school to the beach, from the beach straight and quickly out into the expanse. Outside – according to expert assessment not so far away – is where several frozen ships lay, among them a destroyer. That's where the destination was. But it serves us well to take a good, examining look at Jochen and his four comrades, who all trotted off as glowing runaways, bursting with power, into the horizon. They were Alco, called "Vati," 1.96 meters tall, with a massive appearance, if somewhat primeval, a bit slow, but thanks to his strength and towering height the undisputed master and uncrowned king of the division, although he does not use his powers for anything wrong. Otherwise somewhat slow, but definitely not sleepy and above all he is a person with heart and sensitive emotion. The second one is Jochen's friend and counterpart "Pummel"; perhaps where the heart is concerned the nicest of them all, although one can only guess from the look and sound, since he says very little and especially nothing personal. Jochen's "counterpart", I say, because Pummel is a little clumsy and chubby. He always has too many hands and his body with its slightly moving mass, seems to swim vaguely in space and to sway, whenever Pummel stands still: the big limbs don't have a proper balance. Busso would be the third one: a delicate, noble boy with great, darkly smart and recognizing eyes, which somewhat shyly see the world, but are also a little amused and know how to glint ironically. With him it is almost as if there flowed mental streams upwards from the glow of his eyes, over and above his forehead, while mouth and chin hint at something withered, without luster: the lack of physical fullness, the absence of sensual presence. The educated, smart adult is already perceptibly modeled in the features. One could almost forget the boy in his developing years, or almost the boy at all and only feel something light: the glow of a pure and rich soul. The fourth is different from the others already mentioned; he is urbane, a "young gentleman," who dressed well and was well-groomed, but most of what he is seems to be in what one sees, on the outside. It is also strange that one is tempted to name the price per meter of his good fabrics. And what is too much on the outside, seems to lack within. Therefore, his politeness has something insincere and ugly about it. It seems to prevent a *faux pas* of some sort, or is this judging too harshly? Is there more to him? Is the smooth exterior really just "exterior?" That will show afterwards, after the expedition, because then they will have all undergone a baptism of fire and either passed or failed, even Jochen, who this is actually about and who brings up the rear as now fifth and last.

They now sally forth. It is two o'clock; they have to be back by seven o'clock for dinner, which is why their steps are fast-paced. The march tires them soon; their ankles begin to hurt, because the ice is not the usual smooth ice of the wide meadows. The lake is not exactly regular and equally frozen, but driven pack-ice forms the bulk here in thick irregular layers, then in another spot in a single, thin, often still transparent layer. Walking often turns to climbing and sliding and as they must decide to turn back by 5:25, the ships and the destroyer are still far away out there. The stroll has turned into exertion, the joke turned to seriousness. While they have climbed beachward for half an hour, stumbled and slid, they happen unto a wide gap in the ice, which has formed in the meantime. For the first time fear passes through the boys. They walk up and down the side of the freezing channel, in order to find a connection with the mainland again: without success. The channel stretches endlessly, immeasurably, no matter how far they walk. Perhaps it goes right through the length of the lake. Slowly cold and darkness fall, so that they have to tread carefully to move ahead somewhat; twice, three times one of them walked on innocently and sank in. Alvo was their savior, although Pummel was already up to his knees and Busso up to his hips in the water. That's why they now walk in file, then only the first one will sink in. But the two of them, who were in already, begin to freeze; their clothes turn hard and stiff.

Then they suddenly see how several light beams scan the ice. Now they know that we are looking for them … at one point they stand in the middle of one of those beams, they wave, move, signal … all for nothing. The beam of light can only be searched and shapes in it clearly seen about two kilometers from the land and they are much farther out than that. Time passes. It turns very cold, but high and clear and shining, the almost full moon comes out above them. Its white ethereal light floods everything. Will it help them? They decide to try once again, for a final time to walk out to the destroyer. Since it is frozen in, so they think, the layer of ice must reach right up to it. With great care and very slowly, they walk toward it for a second time. When it is, after several hours, still hundreds, or perhaps less than a hundred meters away, it is over for a second time. Again they stand at a broad channel. Perhaps they are in earshot? Perhaps the guard …? They call, they scream, they holler to the best of their ability – no answer. They burn several matches at once and hold up a stretched out kerchief behind them, in order to improvise a kind of light shade. All in vain. The crew is celebrating Hermann Göring's birthday, the guard is also celebrating … and so hours pass. Midnight comes and then endlessly slowly, dawn and day approach. They now march back, driven by restless, hasty worry, pushing on again landward and rushing almost feverishly toward the firm, the safe. In full daylight again they reach the first great ditch and stand once again before an insurmountable obstacle. But it now no longer measures about just 30 meters across and even wider gaps now appear. From ice to ice, it may be a full two kilometers. Then it dawns on them with harsh realization that this could cost them their lives, and that play and harmless fun have turned into deadly seriousness. Fear shoots icily through their bodies and quietly and fearfully young prayers rise up into the wintery sky.

But not long afterwards – about 8 o'clock in the morning – rescue arrives. An icebreaker works its way out of the harbor. It still hasn't seen them. At once, they run hither and thither, move around anxiously and ebulliently to gain its attention. It works. The boat turns sideways, toward them, comes closer, a ladder is pushed down, they can now climb up and are saved. The clock shows 9:30am. We are immediately notified. The janitor comes into my classroom in the middle of a lesson and whispers in my ear … "An icebreaker" … the class settles down.

Because it is a time of war, there are only a few trains running and they arrive only in the evening. Here they are now, the five of them, full of energy, boldly-daring runaways; and yet they are not. Because in front of us there seem to stand five different humans. They are still wrapped in a thick cloud of icy air, the breath of danger still floats above them. There is still something unusual lingering around their group. I envy their reddened, awed and exhausted faces, the saucer-shaped, feverish eyes, that looked death in the eye … but they keep their composure. The principal of the boarding school talks to them. We are alone: he, they and I. We all know him as a tacit, introverted man, who seems to carry something like a burden of fate: his deep-set eyes, which are piercing and fixed, but only questioning and not informing, stare from behind steel-framed spectacles in a threatening fashion. The bony features could belong to an ascetic, and yet there is a line of kindness above his posture and expression. It seems as if life had him once hard and wild by the shoulders and shook him mercilessly. One expects everything from him, but not what the boys now experience. He wants to speak – and cannot. An experienced, mature man is shaken by anger and emotion, such that his body trembles and the voice obeys only shakily. How may he have spent the night, when the fate of the pupils was still uncertain! Everybody has tears in their eyes; Jochen is the coolest of them all. He has no sense for the tragic. To him the whole thing was just a prank. Of course, it could have gone wrong, but it didn't go wrong. I ask myself not without anger, whether he is really so unemotional, as some say about him. Is he even untouched, where tears would do him honor?

Does he actually lack whole, broad areas of his heart, because of his unbroken thirst for action and soldierly nature? Alvo, who is the speaker, is much more touched. Although he is composed, he is deeply touched. His voice vibrates with many, otherwise inaudible tones; he speaks slowly, haltingly, gently. He wants to mediate, apologize and can't or won't be untrue. His great, natural resilience takes on everything. His fortresses are difficult to shake. His securely built and unused soul, supported by the upstanding

Hans Joachim at Darze (family estate) in the summer of 1940, aged sixteen. Courtesy Gertrud v. Ketelhodt.

physique, carries the wonderful armor of the lively boy, that still protects without exertion. The urbane one is very pale. Firstly and lastly one sees in him the horror. Fear, shivering fear has occupied this body for long hours and is still present in foot and finger. One can also read amazement in the big, always slightly unseeing eyes: he cannot quite grasp that they are now truly safe and the previous night is in the past. He cannot quite cope with the feeling of fatefulness, which was present overly much to pass him by completely, yet too unknown for him to fully grasp it. So he is just shocked and unclearly depressed. Busso stares pale and confused into blankness. He cannot bear looks either now nor in the days to come. We let him go gently, give him time and peace to come to terms with what the sudden and unexpected events of that night has torn apart and shaken. Pummel seems strangely unchanged; that is, he is not untouched, but the experience has not pierced the solid layer of cordial balance, not managed to push aside what always surrounds him protectively. Even the fact that he is the only one with visible consequences, frozen feet, does not alter the picture of the undamaged, who still had to walk through this icy night. Here is a nature that nothing much can push out of balance, that hardly ever gives up the external equanimity and is always cordial and correct.

So the boys are back, they are back in good health, they are back in their full number. Should the shock be punishment enough? Should we, can we punish them, without human measure becoming small and meaningless, where suddenly life overcame death? We waver for a long time. The principal does not want punishment. Such a night is punishment enough, he says. I do not agree. He transfers too much of his own serenity onto the boys. I already see Jochen, how he reads the following day, flattered, seen by all around him taking in the report of his own heroism in the local paper; he enjoys reading it and digests it full of satisfaction. He'd really like to throw himself into a heroic pose. If he had a cap on, he'd push it back into his neck …

We think about it two whole days, and the decision is unusual. Alvo, Pummel and Busso shall not receive punishment; for the other two, we think punishment is deserved. Because, when five do the same, it is five times something different. The fact that we can only agree on two groups reflects the often inevitable simplicity which is so often needed in life: the decision becomes more visible as such and easier to understand. The three more sensitive ones have come to the conclusion that their doings were wrong, when they burdened us with responsibility we were never supposed or expected to have carried. But the parents would have looked for and found the final, the actual guilt with us. Whatever the boys did, they saw themselves involved in a harmless prank, surely … I basically think the same: it was exuberance, a somewhat mad joke. But the unexpected consequences suddenly tore this excursion right to the limits of the tragic and these factors made the boys

guilty. Warned repeatedly, they were aware of the dangers. Their indifference was their mistake; with that they caused an honored adult suffering and much distress and were themselves witnesses to such. This was at the same time their crime and their penance.

The two others didn't seem sufficiently punished by this. We therefore let them choose between corporal punishment or leaving the boarding school – and thereby the circle of friends. Just the boarding school? Surely the school itself! Because nothing can stop the boys from taking board at a private boarding house and carry on attending our school. But of course, they only did wrong against us, against the boarding school, only ignored the repeated and express ban that we had imposed. Despite this, the announcement of their punishment hits them hard. Upset and indignant, they storm into my room after the roll call, this time truly beside themselves. They are forgetting themselves. In the urbane one, his true colors show. He becomes cheeky, almost vulgar, and only a really cutting, a hurtful, hard phrase from me puts him in his place. But even Jochen doesn't know at first what he is saying. In other situations, he is so often a young man; now, as he comes in, he is almost a lout. But this is only an outburst. He is infected. A look keeps him in check. Two people separate themselves from each other. To restore order, I keep him inside and send the other one out.

Now Jochen must listen to the bitter explanation, why he and the well-dressed one enjoy less of our respect than the other three comrades. He must listen to why he counts less, because he, even though our pupil and young friend, means less to us. None of the three who escaped without punishment, I tell him, had read the report about the expedition in the canteen in front of everybody. None of them would have dared to do that; their sense of propriety would have kept them from doing so. Despite having been in mortal danger only twelve hours before, he should not have played so quickly the role of the young hero. I tell him many more such things which occurred during the past few months and weeks; much of it is unimportant; yes, it even appears petty to me to name such things, where a healthy, young comrade has just been given back to us. But still those everyday things show the nature of the student, his attitude, his nature. Jochen understands that. He listens. He has become meek. Through all this criticism, he does feel the healing of the educating spirit, floating above him, that he cannot withdraw from, because he feels his character is being properly determined and guided through it. Perhaps it is such that a human being also accepts the bitter things, when his best forces are pointed out and called dark. Jochen has an understanding of inner direction, he has intuition. But his perception circles basically only around the corporal punishment, of which the boys are not seeing a clear picture in the heat of the moment; they believe it would be carried out by the older students, who usually have supervisory capacity at the boarding school and can dish out minor punishment. I explain to him that the principal and I would be in charge of that. This gives him tangible relief. Despite this he still battles with his feeling of violation and it takes a lot of effort to convince him otherwise.

However, I explain to him the reasons for such childish punishment: "Have you been very grown-up, when you, who have lived by the sea for several years, did not pay any attention at all to the probable consequences? Have you been very grown-up, when you, who are almost still a newcomer, without hesitation began to read about your shining achievement in the rosy light of the printed word, without any shame whatsoever, in front of everybody?" And then I put it to Jochen, the unaffected and passionate comrade, to freely decide whether he wants to leave us, his comrades, if he now still believes that his honor is being violated. He works hard; his eyes are moist, his nose is running, but he clearly utters with a hoarse voice the one word, "No." Then I push my hand through his wiry, wheat blond hair. I did not misjudge him … and from now on, his name is "Jochen."

The human being is a mysterious being. From this moment on, he is my young friend; what's more, I definitely feel that he also clearly feels a turning point: I am to him no longer the educator, just his teacher; I am something different, something more now. The undercurrents of emotion, mysterious and frequently undetected, were veiled in several layers, but unfailingly came together in a dramatic moment.

What else follows is told quickly. The urbane one has quickly contacted his parents' home during this long half hour, and called for the distant protection of the mother, because every sense temporarily left him. Or is it such that one acts in moments of bursting emotions in one's true nature? I send him to the principal. They also talk long and seriously. And see, what a worthy person manages to do: the consideration, the gentleness are compelling, they move him; his mild manner leads him to understanding; his seriousness does not tolerate an inner escape. He demands the whole person and finds him. The urbane one submits; more than that, he justifies the punishment to his mother. Can we, may we expect more than that? No! But even this is not all: late in the afternoon, the other three boys come to us. They come with slow, trudging step and ask for the same punishment that the comrades want to take upon themselves. They cannot bear to get away with it so easily. "*I had a comrade …*"; it shoots through my heart. Oh, you comrades, but we reject their demand completely … slowly the day ends. Later on that evening, we call the twenty boys of the section to an assembly. Their faces are depressed. They all carry the burden, one more than the other, some visibly, others more controlled. The principal speaks, holding back as ever, just somehow pushed back inside, or just without passion. Hesitant to let out what is moving him inside his heart, but still with warmth and the expression of his own deep calmness. He cancels the punishment. "You have submitted," he says and his eyes are sunk deeper than usual, "now I can cancel your punishment" … and the boys sense how much relief this also gives to him. We have reached the end of it. Somehow everybody is grateful and quiet. A dark fate has touched us. What does the principal read the next day as his morning homily? "Now thank we all our God …"

The bond with Jochen has been created. It lasted, however, only a few weeks. Because now that inner urge didn't leave him alone. Ever stronger became his desire "to be part of it," to be there; in short, to be a soldier. At first, his mother laid down the law, which put the brakes on for a time; then she pleaded with him to remain at school. But in time nothing worked anymore. "What belongs to you, you cannot get rid of, and would throw it away immediately," says Goethe, the connoisseur of the human heart. Now his mother pleads in vain, as the nature of her child is so strong and true. So I ask her eventually myself, not to stand in her boy's way. Jochen is allowed to go to a final interview with the regiment. After two days he receives his cabled message: "Entrance granted." We say our goodbyes. Two weeks later it is the exchange of letters that have to replace the human being. "*I am on duty with the volunteers that have just joined, but receive in the evenings extra lessons together with Max Schmeling* [former world heavyweight boxing champion] *at the M.G., M.P.* [machine gun and machine pistol]. *Max Schmeling is in the same platoon with me and at night, we talk about the most interesting problems.*"

Yes, the bravest branch of the service was just brave enough for Jochen. He went to the paratroopers… That all happened in the months of February, March and April 1941. The training was not easy; sweat drops flowed whenever the corporal was not happy. They were often chased here and there and sank dead tired into bed at night. But Jochen never regretted his decision, he never complained, he never even thought that staying at home would have been better.

The war in the Balkans begins. It also turns into a Blitzkrieg. News from Jochen dwindles. On 16 May, he writes a postcard: "*Dear doctor! You are surely cross with me by* now because you haven't heard anything from me for such a long time. It is, however, also a sign that I'm doing very well. In M[isdroy] everybody is surely swimming by now. Many warm greetings from your Jochen." No mention that they have been in transport for over two weeks, as we know from another source, not the slightest indirect hint that things could become serious soon. The older brother, as an officer, can send news again on the 19th; he can also tell us that the operation will begin on the following day. Crete is being attacked. Fate is fulfilled … For three long weeks we hear nothing, not even the mother. That cannot mean anything good, since we have heard that the regiment is already on its way home. At last, a letter from the commander of the regiment arrives, which puts an end to all fearful expectations in one go:

Paratrooper Regiment 1, Iraklion, the 4/6/1941.
Commander.

My very dear Countess!

I deeply regret, having to be the messenger of such devastating news, that during the attack on Crete, all three brothers Wolfgang, Leberecht and Hans Joachim were killed in action …

… The regiment is proud of these three heroes. Their deeds and glory are everlasting. May it serve as consolation to you, my dearest Countess, that these fallen soldiers fulfilled their commitment, which was inherent in their name.

In deepest adoration and constant connectedness …

A paratrooper, who had been in the same platoon as Joachim, later gave us the following details:

Since Jochen's platoon leader especially valued his reliability and his soldierly conduct, he appointed him as his combat messenger. During the attack, Jochen received a serious lung shot as he stood next to his Leutnant. He collapsed immediately yet still attempted to say something. Twice he began: "Leutnant, sir …" and then just: "Sir, Leutn …" A stream of blood, he turned pale as ash and was being carried back. Half an hour later he was gone.

Farewell, blond Jochen! Your beginning was already your end. He, who the gods love …

Note that the description of Hans Joachim's death here differs from the account provided by an eyewitness in Wolfgang's platoon. I have not found any accounts that reconcile these differing reports.

Eventually the news of the loss of three of their favorite sons was to reach the tiny village of Fincken. Gertrud recalls that just as the entire village showed great pride in having three of its young men serving in the celebrated *Fallschirmjäger*, so it was deeply affected by this terrible event. But as the war continued, such losses would become a daily event in towns, cities and villages throughout Germany. Gertrud remembers that the glory associated with such achievements as winning the Iron Cross quickly faded in her family and in others that suffered the loss of one or more sons. As time passed and the reality of total war hit so many families, people began to lose their respect for and loyalty to the armed forces. People who had readily accepted and supported the actions of the armed forces at the start of the war were increasingly confronted with the terrible consequences of sending young men to fight in far away places.

The memorial stone in the Fincken churchyard, dedicated to Wolfgang, Lebrecht and Hans Joachim. It was installed by their sister, Gertrud von Ketelhodt. Author photo.

Soon enough the exploits of the men who took Crete would disappear from the nation's newspapers, magazines and newsreels. Operation Barbarossa, which began on 20 June, was so huge in scale that after the great encirclements of whole Soviet armies and the advances which took the panzers into the heart of the Soviet Union, the casualty lists which grew so quickly once the winter stalemate set in, exceeded anything previously experienced by Germany. The losses on Crete, so deeply felt by the *Fallschirmjäger* and by the families of those who died, would look insignificant against those on the Eastern Front and the sacrifices of families like the von Blüchers

Oberst Bruno Bräuer while on Crete in May 1941. Courtesy Fallschirmjäger archive, military archives, Freiburg.

would be forgotten as the previously unimaginable casualties suffered in Russia affected families all over Germany.

For the men who survived Crete, there were many more battles ahead. By September the 1st and 3rd *Fallschirmjäger* Regiments had been transported to the Leningrad front, where they would be employed in piecemeal fashion rather than as a dedicated, formidable force. Bruno Bräuer, now a *Generalmajor*, and his other officers had expected to be sent to North Africa, but now they were to become part of the massive German forces confronting equally huge Soviet armies. Winter and battle inevitably took a heavy toll and the

1st FJR was returned to Germany in mid-1942 for rebuilding. It was then posted to France where Bruno Bräuer handed over command of his beloved regiment to *Oberstleutnant* Karl-Lothar Schulz. Under their new commander, the regiment returned to Russia, this time to the Smolensk area of operations. In late 1943 the regiment returned to Gardelegen, the garrison town that was its base, underwent re-equipment and received replacement men and then proceeded once again to France. In Avignon a new force was being assembled, the 1st *Fallschirmjäger* Division (previously the 7th *Flieger* Division).

The 5th Regiment served with great distinction in North Africa (Tunisia), while some battalions were employed by Kurt Student in Germany in training and developmental roles. Additional units were sent to North Africa, including the famous "Ramcke Brigade," whose exploits and fighting prowess were regarded with awe even by their enemies. In the end, however, many of these fine soldiers went to prison camps after the surrender of Axis forces in Tunisia in May 1943. In a gesture which epitomizes the esteem and respect in which the *Fallschirmjäger* were held by their opponents, the U.S. Army colonel commanding a prison camp in Texas presented one hero of the final battle in Tunisia with his Knight's Cross, which had been sent to him via the Red Cross.

The Allied invasion of Sicily on 9 July 1943 provided yet another theatre of action for the men of the *Fallschirmjäger* divisions. The XI. *Flieger-Korps* now comprised two divisions, the 1st and the newly formed 2nd Division, under the redoubtable *Generalleutnant* Ramcke. The 1st Division jumped into action on Sicily; one of its regiments was commanded by the now *Oberst* Erich Walther. The various regiments and battalions fought with great distinction and conducted a highly disciplined and very successful withdrawal to the Italian mainland where they fought many hard defensive battles while executing brilliantly conducted withdrawals north. Apart from several notable airborne assaults on Mediterranean islands under Italian control (the Italians having by then surrendered and changed sides), the paratroops served as infantry for the remainder of the war in Italy. Their most famous action was the extended battle for Monte Cassino, where the *Fallschirmjägers'* fighting spirit once again amazed their foes. One of the commanders at Monte Cassino was Karl-Lothar Schulz, the man hand-picked by Bruno Bräuer as his replacement as CO of the 1st Regiment. Also in the role as infantry were the men of the 6th Regiment, which fought in Normandy. There *Major* von der Heydte's men fought with great skill and bravery in the Carentan area.

By this stage of the war (1944) many of the men fighting in *Fallschirmjäger* regiments were not jump-qualified and it is sometimes suggested that, "standards had dropped." In strict terms of the standards required of *Fallschirmjäger* recruits before and during the first year or so of the war, this was true, but it is a tribute both to the leadership of the *Fallschirmjäger* units and to the men who fought under them, that the reputation of the *Fallschirmjäger* as fighters of the highest order was never diminished. Though there was only one jump made before the final surrender (that of von der Heydte's *Kampfgruppe* during the Ardennes offensive

Erich Walther as a general towards the end of the war. Bundesarchiv.

in December 1944), the *Fallschirmjäger* fought strongly to the very end.

Many of the von Blücher brothers' comrades-in-arms were killed, wounded or captured during the battles and campaigns mentioned above, but among those who survived was Gerhard Broder, who fought in Italy (at Monte Cassino) and along the Newa in Russia. *Major* Erich Walther, Wolfgang and Hans Joachim's battalion commander would be awarded the Knight's Cross with Oak Leaves and Swords and go on to survive an extraordinary war. After Crete he fought in Russia, was promoted to *Oberst* and took command of the 4th Parachute Regiment. Later he served in Sicily and at the long battle for Monte Cassino. He was commanding officer of

Battle Group Walther during the fighting at Arnhem and Nijmegen, then he was appointed to command the 2nd Parachute Panzer-Grenadier Division in East Prussia. In January 1945 he was promoted to *GeneralMajor*. He was captured by the Russians at the end of the war and was imprisoned in the former concentration camp at Buchenwald. He died there, apparently of natural causes, in December 1947. It was an ignominious end for such a fine soldier and such a principled and brave man.

Oberst Bruno Bräuer returned to Crete as the garrison commander and a *Generalleutnant* in November 1942. During his time on Crete he was regarded as tough but fair and he tried to ensure that Greek civilians were treated with respect. In 1944 he was appointed to command the 9th

Part Five - Aftermath

Oberst Bruno Bräuer (second from left in dark greatcoat) arrives for the dedication of the original German war cemetery on Crete, in late 1941. The cemetery was at Heraklion, near where the Atsaleniou soccer field now stands. Courtesy Gertrud v. Ketelhodt.

Parachute Division, which was mainly comprised of Luftwaffe ground troops, not Bräuer's beloved paratroopers. They fought in the Ukraine, then took up positions on the Seelow Heights in preparation for the last great Soviet offensive of the war. His division, already weakened by the loss of two battalions in the Ukraine, began to crumble under massive Soviet assaults and desertions severely weakened the division's fighting ability. Bräuer, who had led his men in peace and throughout the war with panache, courage and paternal care, suffered a nervous collapse and was relieved of his command in January 1945.

Once the war ended Bräuer was arrested on war crimes charges, specifically his responsibility for the mistreatment and execution of civilians while he was Fortress commander on Crete. Despite the fact

that he was widely regarded by Germans and Cretans alike as the most humane of Germany's Crete commanders, he was found guilty in an Athens court and was convicted in December 1946. Antony Beevor describes him as a "truly unfortunate man" who, in the end, was held responsible for crimes committed under the regime of another general. He petitioned the court for mercy, stating that, "No innocents have been killed by our orders or intention; only culpable and complicit persons have been affected …" His petition was accepted by the Greek parliament, but rejected by its communist members and ultimately the King of Greece rejected his plea. An unnamed comrade of Bräuer said: "Bräuer was respected and esteemed by the Cretan population as was no other commander. During the war he was able to move amid large gatherings of people during his evening walks on the promenade of

Part Five - Aftermath

A party of soldiers attending the memorial wreath. Courtesy Gertrud v. Ketelhodt.

Chania harbor, unaccompanied by security people and completely alone ..." Despite considerable evidence in his favor, at the age of fifty-four Bruno Bräuer was shot by firing squad on 20 May 1947, the anniversary of the start of the Crete invasion. His body was buried by George Psychoundakis, the famous Cretan resistance fighter and author. Later, with Psychoundakis's support his remains were re-interred at the German Military Cemetery at Maleme, where he lies today among the men whose respect and admiration he earned many times over. He may well have been rough and prickly at times, but he proved himself on many occasions and in different theatres of war, a great leader of men.

GeneralMajor Kurt Student remained with his beloved *Fallschirmjäger* for the rest of the war. He was involved in the planning for Operation Hercules, the anticipated invasion of Malta. In September 1943

Oberst Bräuer laying a wreath at the Fallschirmjäger monument. Courtesy Gertrud v. Ketelhodt.

he was responsible for Operation Oak, the rescue and liberation of Benito Mussolini from Gran Sasso in Italy. While publicized at the time as a *Waffen*-SS operation, the planning was conducted by and the bulk of the personnel involved were *Fallschirmjäger*. Student then assumed command positions in Italy and in France after the Normandy landings in June 1944. When Allied airborne forces mounted Operation Market Garden in the Netherlands in September 1944, Student was appointed to command the First Parachute Army (which then existed largely on paper) to oppose the Allied forces. In early 1945 he was appointed to take command of Army Group Vistula, but before he could assume command he was captured by British troops at Mecklenburg in April. In May he was

charged with mistreatment and murder of prisoners of war on Crete and appeared before a British military tribunal. He was found guilty of three charges and sentenced to five years imprisonment. The Greek government then requested his extradition, but this was declined by the British. Student was released on medical grounds in 1948. Thereafter he lived quietly in the then West Germany, where he remained involved with the welfare of his men and frequently attended veterans' gatherings. He died in 1978 at the age of eighty-eight.

The German War Cemetery at Maleme contains the graves of more than 4,400 men and the memorial wall lists the names of another 360 men whose bodies were never found. At the end of the war there were ten separate cemeteries for fallen German

The Fallschirmjäger monument, with honor guard, on the day of the cemetery's dedication. The words on the monument read: "Only one thing remains forever, the glory of the dead heroes." Courtesy Gertrud v. Ketelhodt.

A view of part of the original cemetery. Wolfgang's grave is the first on the left; Hans Joachim is buried next to him. Courtesy Gertrud v. Ketelhodt.

The Fallschirmjäger memorial outside Chania, erected during the war and still standing, though the diving eagle apparently fell off the pedestal several years ago. Courtesy Lebrecht v. Blücher.

soldiers. Two cemeteries at Chania held 739 graves; Gerani (440); Maleme (893); Galatas (53); Agia (33); Chania-Alikianos (101); Alikianos (93); Heraklion (1,000-1,200); Rethymnon (number unknown). Following an agreement between the Greek and (then) West German governments in the late-1950s, the German War Graves Commission worked for over five years to locate and identify remains and re-inter them at one cemetery, on the heights overlooking Maleme. While the present cemetery was under construction the remains were stored at the Ghonia monastery, near Maleme. The matter of German war graves on Crete is vexed and before permission was granted for the consolidation of cemeteries to begin, it became clear that an unknown number of graves had been destroyed by civilians after the German surrender on the island in 1945. Interestingly, the original *Fallschirmjäger* memorial, a large stone sculpture of the paratroopers' breast badge erected during the war, still stands just outside the town

A view of the German war cemetery looking towards Maleme town and the bay. Author photo.

of Chania. It was to Maleme that Gertrud von Ketelhodt journeyed in October 1974 to be an honored guest at the dedication of the cemetery. She spoke movingly of her three brothers, two of whom were buried alongside each other. Lebrecht's body had been identified and buried by his comrades, but at some point it was lost. Despite extensive efforts to find Lebrecht's body, his remains rest undiscovered and the only reminder of him is his name on the wall of the missing, not far from his brothers' grave.

For the von Blücher family the war had not yet released its grip. Following his release from active service as a result of the deaths of his three brothers (on the direct orders of Adolf Hitler), Adolf transferred to the *Luftwaffe* reserve in 1942 and took over the management and ownership of the family estates at Darze and Kaselin. As well as actively managing the properties he studied forestry and agriculture. He married Gisela Plutte in April 1943 and their daughter Countess Gisela von Blücher was born in March 1944. An all too short period of stability and happiness ended shortly after his daughter's birth, when Adolf became the fourth von Blücher brother to die. On 8 June 1944 he was out hunting on his estates when he came across a trap set by poachers. While dismantling it he was set upon by a group of Russian prisoners-of-war and during the ensuing scuffle Adolf received a gunshot wound in the thigh from his own hunting rifle. Despite hospital treatment he died of an embolism the following day.

The Wall of the Missing at Maleme. Author photo.

Wolfgang and Hans Joachim's joint grave at the Maleme cemetery. Author photo.

Part Five - Aftermath

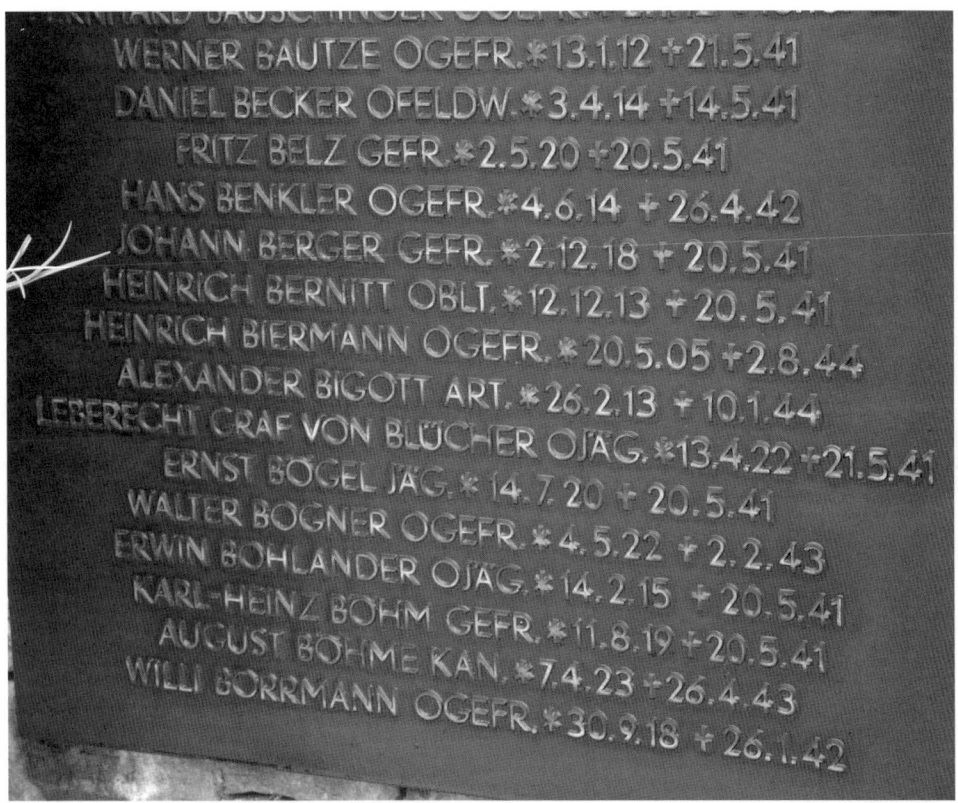

Lebrecht's name is seven from the bottom on the Wall of the Missing. Author photo.

Adolf with his wife Gisela in 1943. Courtesy Lebrecht v. Blücher.

Less than a year later, in April 1945, his widow and baby daughter were forced to flee their property as the Russian armies advanced ever closer. They left Darze in a wagon drawn by four horses, with Gisela's sister-in-law Countess Elisabeth driving the wagon. After eight weeks of constant travel they reached the safety of Hameln, then moved to Eckenhagen in the Rhine province, where they lived in her father's hunting lodge.

The von Blücher children's mother, Gertrud von Nordheim,

Adolf's grave marker in the Fincken churchyard. Author photo.

was also in the line of the Russian advance. She left her home at Posen and found shelter with her sister Charlotte in Mecklenburg, near Wismar. Unfortunately, the rushed departure from Posen and the very limited baggage space that their transport allowed, meant that most family possessions were simply left behind. These included virtually all tangible reminders of the brothers, their possessions, letters, awards and most of the mementos which young men accumulate and keep. Among the few reminders of her sons that their mother kept was Wolfgang's last letter from Athens, the tribute written by Hans Joachim's teacher and a photograph album from which the family photos that appear in this book were taken. To have lost most of those items which are signposts to a person's personality and character and which give substance to their memory is a tragedy for the family and, incidentally, a great loss for this writer. Perhaps some items still exist and rest in collections somewhere. Indeed, in late-2012 Lebrecht von Blücher learned that Wolfgang's Knight's Cross award certificate and its elaborate hand-made leather folder had reappeared. Its whereabouts since 1945 remain a mystery and its current owner wishes to be anonymous, but he has provided a copy of the document for inclusion in this book.

In April Gertrud and Charlotte were forced to take to the road yet again and finally reached Celle, where they lived with her mother-in-law. In September 1945 they moved again to live with her second daughter, Gertrud Michael (later von Ketelhodt) in Lage. That Christmas Gertrud von Nordheim was informed that her husband Ludwig had been taken prisoner by the Russians. When she learned in 1951 that her husband had been sentenced to twenty-five years forced labor she fell seriously ill and remained in poor health until her death in 1966. Her husband was released in 1953.

Gertrud von Nordheim's first daughter, Elisabeth, married Colonel (Ret'd) Hubert von Puttkamer in 1967 and she died in Celle in April 2012. Elisabeth's sister, Gertrud Michael, had lost her brothers and her husband by the time she too was forced to flee from the Russians with her two small daughters. After a long journey from Posen they reached Lage near Neuenhaus where they stayed with her father-in-law. In 1952 Gertrud married Baron Christian Ulrich von Ketelhodt and they settled in Nordhorn. She enjoyed a long working life and is now living in a retirement home in Nordhorn. She is a bright, warm and welcoming lady who gives little hint of the suffering she and her family has endured. She is the last living immediate family member of the von Blüchers of Fincken.

A Reflection

There have been several occasions during the writing of this book when I have wondered whether the lives of three young German aristocrats who died so many years ago can really be of any significance today. As a result of the Crete operation, some 6,368 German servicemen died; by the end of the war the numbers of German military dead exceeded *5.5 million*, of whom approximately 430,000 were members of the *Luftwaffe*. Even these numbers look insignificant alongside the

The author with Gertrud von Ketelhodt in 2012. Author photo.

total estimated deaths as a result of the war, many of which occurred in the then Soviet Union. Of the German servicemen who died, particularly those who fell on the Eastern Front, many have no known grave and their families never discovered where or even how they died. Today these men are largely forgotten, even by their descendants. It is difficult to honor the memory of someone who fought in a war which brought shame and misery to Germany, the only reminder of whom may be a faded photograph of a young man in uniform and whose last resting-place was long ago destroyed by vengeful Russian troops.

I can only say of the three von Blücher brothers that as I searched for information about them (and discovered the utter unreliability of information concerning them on the Internet, where error-filled narratives and "facts" are cut and pasted by well-meaning forum contributors, to the point where you begin to think that if it is on so many websites, then it must be true! At least in the case of the von Blüchers, there is much on the Web that is quite untrue.), I came to know them as human beings. As their stories unfolded, short as they were, they began to give another dimension and considerable depth to the young faces that look out from the photos of them in their *Luftwaffe* uniforms. As I uncovered more, the faces became more than just black and white images, they filled out into young men who had real lives, however short.

In many ways they appear to be typical young men of their time. Wolfgang was not

Wolfgang in 1940, following the award of his Knight's Cross at the age of twenty-three. Courtesy Gertrud v. Ketelhodt.

an academic and he loved the outdoor life in the country, a life that farm management provided. He had drifted into several jobs before he found his true calling of farming and forestry. As previously noted, he was determined to take responsibility for his family from a young age and even then, according to his sister Gertrud, he was the "general" of the family. But his pre-war service in the cavalry reserve and then his training as a paratrooper gave him a new passion. It provided adventure, challenges and opportunities to travel which a farmer's life could not have matched. Fortunately, the personal qualities that led him to take responsibility for the remaining family estates were easily transferable to the military. He had a great sense of duty and a determination to be a leader from the front, one who does everything he asks his men to do. These qualities were equally evident in his family and in his *Fallschirmjäger* platoon. Whenever his leadership was tested, his steadfastness, his courage and his skills all came to the fore. Wolfgang was the sort of combat leader who could inspire total loyalty from his men, men who, even in a life and death situation, would stay with him to the end.

Lebrecht, the budding engineer and lover of literature and music who disappeared so completely on 20 May 1941 that there was nobody left after the battle to tell his story, remains the least knowable of the brothers. His body remains missing (despite the fact that he was buried and a photo of his grave was taken soon after the fighting had concluded) and there is of him only a name on a wall, with no descriptions of his final minutes to give some certainty as to how he died. He was, according to his sister, a young man of great promise, talented in diverse interests, sensitive and with a brilliant smile. Perhaps one day his remains will be discovered and he will join his brothers.

And Hans Joachim, Jochen, the youngest, the young daredevil who just wanted to join his brothers in the paratroops, is probably the one about whom most can be discovered, thanks to the remarkably revealing memoir written by his teacher. He was a very strong youngster, both physically and emotionally, greatly attracted to the glamorous life of the *Fallschirmjäger*, but one whose character and personality, as revealed by his teacher, suggested a boy with a great deal more depth than his exploits at school might indicate. His final act, his last daredevil exploit was to risk his own life to save his brother. And he was just a boy when he died.

However brief their stories, Wolfgang, Lebrecht and Hans Joachim were by all accounts young men of integrity and purpose. Whether they really were representative of their generation in Germany is impossible to say, but all that I have learned about them leads me to believe that they were admirable young men who were greatly loved and respected within their family and by their comrades in the paratroops. They were all drawn to action with the *Fallschirmjäger* by youthful enthusiasm and the younger two by the example set by the older brother whom they idolized; and, of course, they had been taught from their earliest school days to believe that their destiny lay in devoting themselves to serving the Fatherland and if necessary dying for it.

Everything I had discovered about the brothers was reinforced and given additional texture and color when I visited Germany in the course of researching this book. First, I spent a memorable day with their charming sister, Gertrud, whose initial wariness about just how I would be portraying her brothers soon gave way to expansive and spirited answers to my questions. She is a remarkable lady and I felt greatly privileged to be speaking with the last von Blücher sibling. She retained vivid memories of each of her brothers, though the combination of the passing of over seventy years and the fact that the siblings saw much less of each other once the war began, limited the depth of her knowledge of them. Like so many of her generation she is stoical about the losses she and her family endured, but the great love she retains for her brothers was constantly apparent as she reminisced.

Next, I enjoyed several days staying next to their early childhood home at Fincken, in the lakes district north of

Part Five - Aftermath

Lebrecht in Celle, 1939. Courtesy Gertrud v. Ketelhodt.

Berlin. Walking around the extensive grounds of the *schloss*, looking out over the lake where the von Blücher children had learned to swim and rowed their boats and meeting the descendants of the country-folk who spent early childhood years with them, gave me a real sense of the roots of the family. It was not difficult to imagine adventuresome brothers and sisters spending their days exploring, learning and testing their courage in the woods and on the water that surrounds the family home. I found it a strange, yet very heart-warming experience to walk along the same garden paths and lakeside beaches that the von Blücher children had frequented so many years ago. It was not hard to imagine the near-idyllic existence they must have enjoyed when they lived in Fincken, nor was it difficult to appreciate how being so close to nature would have helped to shape their outlooks and interests. Much of their growing up occurred away from the family estate, but anyone who comes from such a beautiful part of rural Germany must never lose their attraction to it.

From Fincken, I travelled south to Freiburg, where I was granted access to the *Fallschirmjäger* archives, held at the military archives located just outside the city. There I immersed myself in the Crete operation and in the written records of the men who led the von Blüchers into action. Documents, photographs, diaries, contemporary publications and maps all added detail and color to the story of these men. As any researcher knows, there is a special feeling to reading the actual documents that concern the subjects of your research. Seeing the signatures, still in strong blue or black ink, of Student, Bräuer and Walther and handling the faded and brittle documents, maps and photographs takes you back to that time in a very concrete way. Far from being dusty and distant, archives can transport the researcher back to when "history" was real life. Certainly, I felt that and I did all I could to use the archives to shine light upon the planning and execution of the Heraklion battles that took the brothers' lives. With a newfound clarity to my understanding of the battles for Heraklion airport it was now time to walk the ground.

And so I flew to Crete, much as Wolfgang, Lebrecht and Hans Joachim had done (though a good deal more comfortably), from Athens on a late May afternoon, with skies clear enough for me to gaze on the dramatic islands which so suddenly appeared out of the sea on the short flight. We were much higher than the Ju 52s flew of course, but the view must have been just as wonderful for the men in 1941, even if their minds were very much focused on the mission ahead of them.

Unintentionally, but very fortuitously, I happened to arrive a few days before the anniversary of the deaths of the brothers so I planned my time on Crete to ensure that I would visit the cemetery at Maleme on the 21st of May (Lebrecht was actually killed on the 20th). Before then I wanted to try to find the area where Wolfgang and Hans Joachim died (the area just to the west of the airport where Lebrecht was killed is now built up). To guide me I had a photocopy of a hand-drawn map I came across in the archives and which was an appendix to an after-action report. It gave a position for Wolfgang's platoon's final stand, but had no topographical reference points other than the coastline, some hills, the coastal road and the airport. Various books about the battle that I had consulted also indicated where that battle took place, but confusingly, their maps placed Wolfgang at different locations. In the end, I decided to use the map from the archives as my primary source, given that it was drawn very soon after the battle and with input from those who were there. With map in hand I set off by taxi to the Greek Air Force base that adjoins the Heraklion airport. My reading of the map suggested that Wolfgang's last battle occurred on or near what is now the base. This was fortunate as much of the land on the base has been left undeveloped since the war. However, a diligent and well-armed gate guard stopped me from strolling through the base with map in hand. No amount of pleading would change his mind, but he became intrigued with my mission and suggested

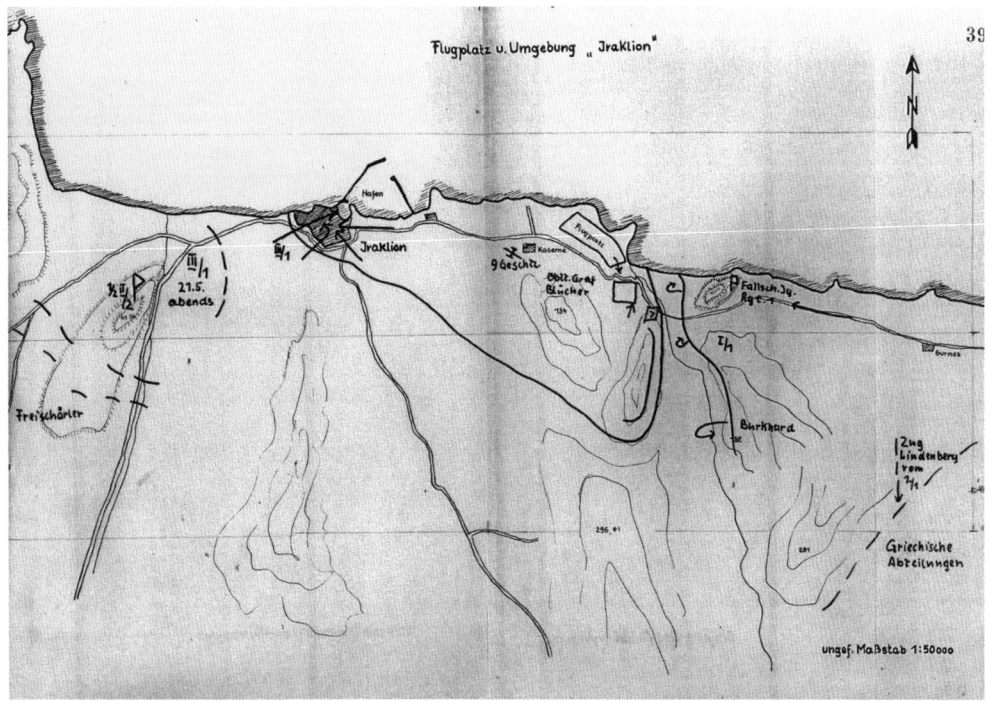

The hand-drawn map which accompanied the after-action report referred to and quoted from in Part 3. This map helped the author to locate the position of Wolfgang's platoon when it was surrounded by the British on 20/21 May 1941. Courtesy Fallschirmjäger archive, military archives, Freiburg.

that I take the taxi to the other side of the base, close to where the map suggested the battle against the Black Watch had taken place. He also mentioned with a smile that although photography of the base was forbidden, the area was largely deserted … So, with a bemused and somewhat reluctant taxi driver off I went on the coastal road to the other side of the base. Once there, it was difficult to pinpoint any positions on the German map, but the coastal road was drawn on the map and its distinctive curves, unchanged to this day, led me to an area that had to be near the battle-site. I took a few photos and returned to the taxi, still not convinced that I was in exactly the right spot. I looked again at the map and then borrowed the driver's GPS device. Holding both I navigated him to where the coast road appeared to come closest to where Wolfgang died, according to the map. A dead-end road which branched off the coast road led up to a desolate and windswept hill-top, which could finally be reached only by walking along a steep and winding track. At the end of the track were several large and aggressive looking dogs chained up (at this point the driver returned to his car) and it was obvious that the area was used as a holding area for sheep and goats. There were a few rundown old sheds, but mostly it was a rocky and uneven landscape with occasional small bushes. As I walked all over the hill-top I tried to get

The battlefield where Wolfgang and his platoon fought, as it is today. The prominent hills in the background are the Two Charlies, from which Australian troops watched in amazement and then fired upon the paratroopers as the first landings were made. Author photo.

my bearings by taking a number of photos looking towards prominent landmarks, such as the Two Charlies. It was beginning to rain as I looked around for the last time and walked as far as I could without driving the dogs into a frenzy. Just before returning to the taxi I took one last shot towards two prominent and unusually shaped hills to the southwest. I was still not sure whether I had been at or near the site of the battle, but if the map was accurate I should have been close; and for some reason during the taxi ride back into town I sensed that I had been drawn to that desolate patch of ground in a way which I still cannot explain.

The next day I drove to Maleme. It was the 21st of May 2012, seventy-one years to the day that Wolfgang and Hans Joachim were killed. My journey to discover who they were would end, appropriately, at their resting place.

The German military cemetery at Maleme stands on the slopes overlooking the airfield that was the scene of so much hard fighting in 1941. At the entrance is a small display area and one of the information panels relates the story of the deaths of the von Blücher brothers. Today the hill-side is a serene place, beautifully maintained and understated with its low grey stone walls and flower-edged paths. At the center of the cemetery stands the wall on which the names of the missing are inscribed. Around this, in long rows and surrounded by local

The same area as in the previous photo, but looking towards the eastern end of the airport. It must have seemed tantalizingly close to Wolfgang and his men. Author photo.

wildflowers are the graves. This carpet of multi-colored flowers is most striking and beautiful. Soon I found Wolfgang and Hans Joachim lying together among their comrades. I had brought with me a small bunch of yellow flowers (yellow for the collar tabs of the *Fallschirmjäger* blouses) with a card attached, noting that this was the anniversary of their deaths. I laid it on the gravestone and let my mind revisit all that I had learned about these three young men. It was a most moving moment and quite unexpectedly, I was overcome by the accumulated emotion of the lengthy and often difficult journey to find the brothers; I had come to know Wolf, Lebs and Jochen as well as was possible seventy years after their deaths and they had become real people to me, not just names on a page. I thought about the utter waste of such fine youngsters, of how bravely they had died, of what they might have been had they survived the war. I have so often stopped working on the book and wished that I could have sat down with each of them, shared a drink and just talked. Standing with them, my mind reflected on these young men whose hopes and plans for their futures died with them when they fell on the flinty soil of an island which now claims them. And so, at this peaceful spot so far from their homeland, once the scene of such bitter fighting for Maleme airport, Wolfgang, Lebrecht, Jochen and I met at last.

The western edge of the airport, where Lebrecht and his company landed. The hill at right is one of the Two Charlies. Author photo.

There was one last discovery, an astonishing one, from my journey to Crete. Several weeks after I returned home, Lebrecht von Blücher sent me copies of photographs from Gerhard Broder's book. Mr. Broder and his publisher had given me permission to use them and one was the last picture taken of Wolfgang (not published in Mr. Broder's book). Another was a shot taken of his first grave, on the battlefield. According to Gerhard Broder, he was buried where he fell. As I looked closely at this photo I noticed the very distinctive outlines of two hills behind the grave. My mind suddenly flashed back to my last minutes on that desolate hilltop near Heraklion airport and I quickly went to the photos I had taken there. I was amazed when I looked closely at the last shot I had taken: those same hills were in the background, looking exactly as they had in Mr. Broder's photo; my photo was taken from the same point of view and angle as in the photo of the grave; and the hills were at the same distance from the camera. My heart raced for a few seconds when it dawned on me that without realizing it at the time, I had stood within a few meters of where Wolfgang had been killed and then buried. Somehow, I had stumbled across not just the site of the battle, but the very place of his death. A natural skepticism keeps me from suggesting that I was meant to find this place, but part of me would like to believe that something beyond my understanding brought me to that spot.

When I look at their formal portraits in uniform now I see in their shining eyes and purposeful yet enigmatic expressions, good young men who bravely served their country. At this distance of course, over seventy years, one cannot *really* know such young men. Even their sister, Gertrud, admits that she never knew them very well, but laments the fact that so young were Lebrecht and Jochen when they died that they had never even had girlfriends. There is so much more about them that I would

Wolfgang von Blücher's first grave, on the battlefield where he fell. Courtesy Paul Bernhard.

like to know: their hopes and dreams for the future, of course; their passions; their thoughts about their country and its leader; their thinking on so many subjects. But these all died with them and what we know now, as recorded in this book, is probably all that we will ever really know about Wolfgang, Lebrecht and Hans Joachim von Blücher. It is not enough and I think they deserve more, but it is more than is known about most of their dead comrades-in-arms. The von Blücher brothers' story is just one small tile in the vast mosaic of life stories that together comprise the Second World War. But, however insignificant, this tile has its own distinct form and outline, color and texture; it is integral to the whole and without it the mosaic would be the lesser.

The same area today. Note the distinctively shaped hills in the background of both photos. Author photo.

A section of the German war cemetery at Maleme, a place of peace for the men who fell on Crete. Author photo.

Acknowledgements

The genesis for this book was an article by Will Fowler in the May-June 2011 edition of *The Armourer* magazine, commemorating the 70th anniversary of the Crete invasion. A sidebar in his story told of the von Blüchers and gave a brief outline of their tragic demise. Raymond Watson's assistance was acknowledged at the bottom of the sidebar and through the kind assistance of Irene Moore, then the magazine's editor, I was able to e-mail Raymond. I had found the von Blücher story quite fascinating and wondered whether there was enough information about them to justify a longer article. Raymond, who turned out to be a frequent visitor to Crete and a wonderful source of information, encouraged me to pursue the story. I greatly appreciate both his initial encouragement and his continuing interest and support.

So began an intriguing, often frustrating but ultimately immensely rewarding journey of discovery. I began, as we so often do these days, on the Internet. As Wolfgang had been awarded the Knight's Cross I managed to find out more about him quite easily – there are various sites which list and document all Knight's Cross winners – and there were several brief mentions of his younger brothers. Along the way I found a couple of sites devoted just to the von Blücher brothers. One of these, a shrine-like site in the Bahasa Indonesia language, is really quite bizarre and I did not regret that my understanding of that language is very limited. It quickly became evident that much of what was told about the von Blüchers and endlessly repeated on various websites devoted to the study of every possible aspect of the German war machine in the Second World War, is simply wrong. In most cases, this is the result of one person innocently cutting and pasting from one source to provide information on another site. Unfortunately, the errors on the original remain and with repeated posting, become accepted as fact. The quality of these sites varies considerably, but for those who have not visited them, they are real eye-openers. Some contributors seem to spend much of their lives tracking down arcane "facts" about obscure soldiers of the *Wehrmacht*. Much of their information is fascinating, but it is difficult to assess the accuracy of most of the content. These sites also tend to attract extremely opinionated individuals who are quick to criticize other contributors and who assume a position of unassailable authority. Their writings are often interesting, but researchers should treat all information on these sites as being untested.

Having quickly realized the limitations of the Internet in this area of research, I turned to tracking down any members of the von Blücher family who may have been able to assist. As I don't read German, this too was a time-consuming and ultimately fruitless task. As a last ditch measure I turned to Ancestry.com (where perhaps I should started!) and sent messages to anyone who appeared to have von Blücher connections. Eventually I found a family tree on which the brothers were listed and I sent an e-mail to Barbara Smith in the UK, who was the keeper of the family tree. She responded very positively and put me in touch with a Michael Blücher in Germany. He was of a different branch of the family, but was kind enough to link me with the von Blücher family historian – he had recently published a history of the family from 1914 (an earlier volume related the family history before then) – who was more closely related to the brothers.

Lebrecht von Blücher, of Merzhausen near Freiburg, turned out to be the single most significant contributor to my research. Not only did he know of the brothers, but he knew their sisters, who still lived in northern Germany. He offered to contact them on my behalf and although the eldest sister sadly passed away shortly before I was able to visit her, through his liaison work I was able to spend a most fruitful day with Gertrud von Ketelhodt (née von Blücher). When I visited Germany to meet Gertrud and to do other research at the military archives close to their home I stayed with Lebrecht and his delightful wife Gerhild. I cannot begin to thank them enough for their most generous hospitality. Lebrecht has assisted me with translations, tracked down Mr. Gerhard Broder and spoke with him on my behalf, discovered and scanned most of the photographs which appear in this book (many of which have never been published before), answered my sometimes daily emails and generally supported my research and writing in every way possible. I owe him a huge debt of gratitude and I am delighted to have both Lebrecht and Gerhild as good friends.

My good friend Kim Walton, like Lebrecht von Blücher, has been invaluable in the support he has been able to provide me from Germany. He drove me from his home in Bremen to Nordhorn, some 200 kilometers distant, where Gertrud von Ketelhodt lives. In addition, his colleague at the International School of Bremen, Linda Gibbins, accompanied us and acted as interpreter for my interview with Gertrud. Linda and Gertrud established a warm rapport and I am certain that without Linda's presence the interview would have been far less productive. Kim was also instrumental in arranging for a senior student at his school, Darius Matuschak, to become involved in translating the transcript of the interview with Gertrud. Darius was fascinated by the von Blüchers' story from the start and he worked most diligently and enthusiastically to produce the final translation. Without his dedicated work my understanding of the von Blüchers' early life would have been very limited and I am most grateful to him for his interest and skills. Markus Neumann, a teacher of German at the school, helped with some tricky German words and possible connotations for them. Kim has helped in a myriad of small ways and like Lebrecht has received a constant barrage of emails from me, mostly requesting his help. He has been most generous of his time, even when he couldn't really spare it and without his contributions and those of Lebrecht this book would simply not have seen daylight.

Also in Germany, my warmest thanks go to *Freifrau* Gertrud von Ketelhodt. This remarkable ninety-one-year-old lady spent most of a day with Kim, Linda and me and she proved to be a most charming and informative interviewee. Her memories of her brothers and their time growing up add a very special dimension to the book. I wish to thank also her son Ulrich von Ketelhodt, who facilitated my visit to his mother. I still find it remarkable that I was able to speak at length with the last living sibling of those three men.

It was at Lebrecht von Blücher's suggestion that I also visited Fincken, the site of the former von Blücher family estate. My lack of German and the almost total lack of English among the village's residents made for an interesting and challenging stay, but I cannot offer enough praise for the hospitality and help given by all with whom I came in contact. The staff at the *Kavalierhaus* Hotel, situated in one of the estate's original buildings, went out of their way to meet my requests and answer questions. They arranged for the translation of various historical booklets for me and put me in touch with the *Bürgermeister*, Erich Nacke. He didn't speak English but he was able to give me a most interesting tour of the village and then arrange for a friend of his, Hans Padzinski to take me through the old von Blücher home. Its owner lives abroad and the house has been shut for a number of years, but I was able to wander through the house, literally from cellars to roof space, at leisure and Herr Padzinski was the source of some interesting facts about the house. I am most grateful to the people of Fincken for their patience and their willingness to help a stranger in need!

I made contact with the German Paratroop Veterans' Association early in my research and they have been most supportive of my project. In particular I would like to thank Hans Oehler and Colonel (Ret'd) Steffen Rhode for their suggestions, advice, help with information and in particular for allowing me to have access to the extensive *Fallschirmjäger* archives held at Freiburg. The Association archivist, Falko Heitmann kindly arranged for me to gain access to the archive in Freiburg. The documents, photographs and other articles in this collection have been collected over many years and form an invaluable historical record of the *Fallschirmjägers'* war. They also put me in touch with veteran Gerhard Broder, whose photographs and recollections enhance this book. *Glück Ab!* I appreciate the generosity of Paul Bernhard, the publisher of Mr. Broder's book, for permission to use photographs from that book. I am also most grateful to Mr. Skye Moog, with whom Lebrecht von Blücher made contact and who provided and permitted me to use many of the photographs in this book. For the fine photographs of Wolfgang's Knight's Cross certificate, I wish to thank most sincerely Mr. Andreas Thies, proprietor of Auktionshaus Andreas Thies EK. Mr. Thies learned of the book and made known to me that he was aware of the existence of the document, then negotiated with its owner (to whom I also give my thanks), who wishes to remain anonymous. The result is a photographic record of a piece of family history, thought lost forever some seventy years ago.

The staff at the German Military Archives in Freiburg could not have been more co-operative and generous with their time. Mr. Achim Koch and his colleagues made my days spent at the archives rewarding and enjoyable; I am most grateful to them.

There are others whose names I do not know, but who, through their kindness made my work easier and more productive: the front desk staff at the Grand Elysée Hotel in Hamburg, who helped me complete the necessary paperwork (in German) to gain admission to the military archives; the translators at Wits University in South Africa who produced fine translations of all the written material in German I had accumulated; the superintendent of the German War Cemetery at Maleme who was most kind and understanding; the Greek Air Force guard at the main gate to the Heraklion base and the taxi driver who lent me his GPS navigation device on the day I found the site of Wolfgang's last stand; the front desk staff at the Galaxy Hotel in Heraklion, who went out of their way to assist me.

So many people have contributed in very different ways to the writing of this book. Many others have become fascinated by the story I have told and have been sources of encouragement and motivation whenever I felt that I would never find out enough to justify writing a book. In fact, one of the great discoveries I have made during the course of researching and writing is that there are many very good people one comes across while working at such a project, people who have been prepared to devote considerable time and energy to supporting, in various ways, my work. To all of them, my deepest thanks and appreciation for your support. Of course, any errors in the book are mine alone.

I have tried to be diligent in keeping a list of names of those who have helped me, but I am sure that I have neglected some. If I have, my apologies and my thanks!

Bibliography

Bailey, Ronald H. and the Editors of Time-Life Books, Partisans and Guerrillas (World War II Series, Vol. 12), New York, 1978.

Beevor, Antony, Crete: The Battle and The Resistance, Penguin Books, London, 1991.

Bond, George, Crete: The Graveyard of the Fallschirmjäger, Nimble Books LLC, USA, 2010.

von Blücher, Lebrecht, Geschichte der Familie von Blücher 1914-2003, Blücher Verlag, 2003 (in German) ISBN 3-934249-01-9.

Broder, Gerhard and Paul Bernhard (Editor), Guerre Mondiale Contre Moi, Dieter Friess Publishing, 2009, 2nd edition (in German).

Christensen, Ben, The 1st Fallschirmjäger Division in World War II: Years of Attack, Schiffer Publishing USA, 2007.

Die Ritterkreuzträger der Deutschen Wehrmacht: Tiel II: Fallschirmjäger, Franz Thomas und Günter Wegman. Biblio-Verlag, Germany, 1986.

Fergusson, Bernard, The Black Watch and The King's Enemies, Collins, London, 1950.

von Ketelhodt, Gertrud (neé von Blücher), interview with author, 5 May 2012.

Kurowski, Franz, Jump Into Hell: German Paratroopers in World War II, Stackpole Books, USA, 2010.

Laffin, John and the Editors of Time-Life Books, Greece, Crete and Syria (Australians at War Series, Vol. 13), Time-Life Books Australia, 1989.

Müller, Günther and Scheuering, Fritz, Sprung über Kreta, Stalling Verlag, Oldenburg 1944. (in German)

Nasse, Jean-Yves, Fallschirmjäger in Crete, Histoire & Collections, Paris 2002.

Panayiotakis, George I., The Battle of Crete, Heraklion, 1993.

Pöppel, Martin, Heaven and Hell: The War Diary of a German Paratrooper, The History Press Ltd, UK, 2010.

Quarrie, Bruce, Fallschirmjäger: German Paratrooper 1939-45, Osprey Publishing, Oxford, 2001.

The Editors of Time-Life Books, Conquest of the Balkans (Volume in The Third Reich Series), Alexandria VA, 1990.

Other Sources

German Military Archives, Freiburg, Germany.

Gertrud von Ketelhodt, interview with author, May 2012.

Letter from and interview (telephone) with Gerhard Broder (conducted by Lebrecht von Blücher), August 2012.

www.ritterkreuzträger-1939-1945.com provided biographical details on senior Fallschirmjäger officers.

www.waroverholland.nl, provided many of the details of the battle for the Dordrecht Bridges.

Skye J. Moog Collection (photographs)

Mr Andreas Thies (photographs)

German Ranks and Allied Equivalents

German	British/Commonwealth/USA
Jäger	Rifleman/Private
Gefreiter	Lance Corporal
Obergefreiter	Corporal
Unteroffizier	Sergeant
Oberjäger	Sergeant
Unterfeldwebel	Staff Sergeant
Feldwebel	No direct equivalent; usually platoon leaders
Oberfeldwebel	Company Sergeant Major/Warrant Officer
Leutnant	Second Lieutenant
Oberleutnant	First Lieutenant
Hauptmann	Captain
Major	Major
OberstLeutnant	Lieutenant Colonel
Oberst	Colonel
General der Fallschirmjäger	Lieutenant General of Airborne Troops
GeneralMajor	Major General

Note

This is not a history; it is an attempt to tell the story of three young men who died over seventy years ago. While I have relied on official documents and established sources for the most part, I have also made use of private letters, reminiscences and personal recollections. I am very much aware that such factors as the passage of more than seventy years, the unique perspective of a man in combat, whose direct knowledge of a battle is usually and necessarily limited to his own terrifying patch of the field, the desire to tell what one has come to believe is true, may result in the presentation of events in ways which are at odds with other contemporary or recollected accounts. I have no reason to doubt the accuracy of any of the sources used in this book, but I am also conscious of the vagaries of memory over many years.